MESSIANIC 101: THE ESSENTIALS

Arthur Bailey

©2017 Arthur Bailey Ministries

MESSIANIC 101: THE ESSENTIALS

By Arthur Bailey
Arthur Bailey Ministries
PO Box 49744
Charlotte, NC 28277

Published and produced in the United States of America
By Higher Heart Productions for Arthur Bailey Ministries
ISBN: 978-1-5450287-4-2
Library of Congress Control Number: 2017904964

© 2017 Arthur Bailey Ministries. All Rights Reserved. No part of this book may be reproduced, shared, or transmitted by any means without permission from the author.

For more information visit www.ArthurBaileyMinistries.com

This book is designed to compliment Arthur Bailey Ministries videos and/or published teachings. Words in brackets [ ] are typically added for clarification by the editor and publisher.

TABLE OF CONTENTS

PART ONE: IN A NUTSHELL 5
    The Essentials of Our Faith.. 18
    Circumcision Through Abraham 34

PART TWO: WE ARE DISCIPLERS 37
    Keeping the Sabbath 45
    Faith Comes By Hearing.. 46
    Dietary Law, Clean and Unclean 55
    Keeping the Feasts 69
    The Essentials of Our Faith In Conclusion 73

OTHER FINE TEACHINGS 75

PART I: IN A NUTSHELL

Folks have said to me:

"You know, you need to give it to me in a nutshell."

Well, I'm going to try to do a "nutshell teaching" today, if there is such a thing. As more and more people's eyes are opened to the faith once delivered to the saints and as new believers are being added to the family, it is really important that they get started on the path the right way.

I know that for me personally, it took a couple of years to figure things out. During that time in those couple of years, I had allowed certain things in my spirit. Let me tell you something folks. Once you've heard something, you can't "unhear" it. You can't unhear what you've heard.

Now, you can put something in your mouth and you can spit it out, but the taste of it is still there. It takes awhile for you to get that taste out of your mouth, just as it takes awhile sometimes to get a false teaching out of your spirit. I heard some things. As I go back and look at some of the teachings that I did, because of the things that I heard and the things that were deposited in me; I shared and taught those things.

I remember the first time. I came home and wanted to bring in the Sabbath with my family the way I'd been taught. And of course you know, you've got to light the candle. The woman of the house is supposed to pray the prayer. She is supposed to put the tallit over her head and do all of this [waves hands] and usher in the Sabbath and pray that Sabbath prayer.

Let me tell you something, ladies and gentlemen. I got that from this book [holds up a book]. Now, when I came into the Messianic faith, I was handed several books; especially when they found out that I was a pastor and that I was transitioning from Sunday to the Sabbath. [Arthur holds up another book.] This is the *Messianic Jewish Manifesto*.[1]

I've got so many books at home. Folks were sending me books. It was like I was the new (how would I put it?) exotic animal in the zoo. Everybody wanted to come and see this new animal. I will tell you that a pastor who transitioned from Sunday to Sabbath in the Messianic faith is a big "to do." I had people travelling from far and wide just to get a view of this spectacle.

As believers who have been on this way, we have a responsibility to new believers to be a disciple, to be a mentor, to be a coach or whatever you want to call it. You see, we need to learn with the idea that we are going to teach. For you to learn just to have knowledge and information really does very little good. That is because now you just have information and that makes you an "expert."

I was taught early on that an expert is somebody from out of town. I mean, you don't know them and if they sound like they know what they're talking about, they "know more" than the folks who you are familiar with. This is what they say about the people that you're familiar with:

> *"A prophet is without honor save in his own country."*

It amazed me that when I was in the Christian Church and even in the Messianic community, that a minister could come in and preach the *exact* same message the pastor preached last week and all of a sudden folks got a revelation. It's like:

> *"Wow! We've never heard such stuff! [or things]"*

And the pastor is over there saying something like:

---

[1] By David Stern.

> *"What? I preached the same thing. It's the same thing I just preached last week!"*

But because people are familiar and the expert came from out of town, all of a sudden there's a line. There is a line there with people who want to shake the guest minister's hand. Pastor stands by the door and folks go out of all of the side doors.

> *"Aw, we know him. Let the new people shake his hand. We've shook his hand enough."*

Anyway, you need to learn with the idea that you are going to teach. That means that you have to make sure that what you are learning is right. That's because if you learn wrong, you're going to do what? You're going to teach wrong. So you have to learn with the idea that what you are learning, you are going to teach.

One of the philosophies about retention is that *you have to share what you've received.* If you don't share what you've received, it just becomes information that now gets buried with new information. Pretty soon you start forgetting more than you're learning.

New believers to the faith have a lot of questions. They don't want to mess it up; especially if they've been in the "old" way. They have come to realize that they have spent most of their lives learning things that weren't true. They don't want to go through that again, so now they don't want to take up or pick up anything without testing it and making sure that it's solid.

Sometimes we may not know how to explain things, especially if we are new ourselves or are new to certain information. The way you can verify it and get it rooted in your spirit is by practice. You see, if you don't practice loving (for example), you just have knowledge about love.

You could say that YeHoVaH loves the unlovable all you want, but if you don't have the ability to love the unlovable, what good is that? Typically the people who are unlovable are the ones who have wronged us. It's easy to love people you like. It's hard to love people you don't like.

They don't want to mess it up. Unfortunately there are too many teachers teaching new believers the traditions of men instead of the true Gospel of the Kingdom.

I'm going to tell you something folks. This is just some of the stuff that I've retained. [Arthur holds up a book.] I've got a *Messianic Siddur, The Essential Believer's Siddur* and *The Messianic High Holiday Siddur*. These are prayer books – prayer books that you pray on specific days. Here is *The Messianic Shabbat Siddur*. This is the prayer book that you use only on the Sabbath day. Here is another one.

These are all books on how you're "supposed" to keep the Sabbath. [Arthur holds up a handful of books.] All of these books are written by Jewish wannabes. [He holds up several more books.] And these are written by Jews. Actually, I take that back. These three are written by Jews as well. You might ask:

"Now, why are you bringing all of this up?"

It's because of this. Do I need these books to practice my faith? [No.] You answered correctly.

Today there is as much confusion surrounding being Messianic as there is in denominational Christianity. We are going to clear up some of this confusion and help people who are coming into the faith to get started on the right track. That's my goal. As I said earlier, this message is not an attack on anyone, but because of some of the content, it may appear that way.

I'm not here to attack anyone, but if someone has started a belief and other people incorporate that belief, then what you have is a majority speaking some of the same things. This means that if all of these folks are speaking "this," then it "must" be true.

If we're going to truly test, we have to test according to the word and not according to the stuff we've been taught. That is because if we've been taught things that are not grounded in the word and we're taught something that is contrary and from the word that we've been taught, then what are we going to do? Unfortunately too many people hold onto the things that they've been taught, regardless to what you show them in the word.

We must stick to facts and not traditions. Too many people prefer traditions over facts, even when the scriptural facts are presented in a clear and concise way. We're going to do some of that today and hopefully folks will let go of the traditions that are contrary to fact.

"I don't want you to be ignorant."

Paul wrote this to the congregations that he started. He said:

"I would not have you to be ignorant brethren concerning certain things."

I certainly don't want you to be ignorant brethren concerning certain things today. You have to understand that the prophets prophesied to the people of their day. Some of the prophecies that they spoke went beyond their lifespan, but they were specifically speaking to the people of their day.

The apostles and the disciples were speaking to the people of their day. They had an understanding of the culture. They had an understanding of the language. They didn't know the language that we live in today, nor did they live in the culture that we live in today.

So, how do you speak to a people in today's culture and in today's language from the Bible that was written and given to us over 2,000 years ago? Now we need *interpretation*. We need *proper interpretation*. That's exactly what we're teaching on Thursdays as it relates to biblical hermeneutics: the art and science of properly interpreting the scripture.

When I came into the Messianic faith, I didn't realize that I was coming into Messianic Judaism. That's what I came into. I started hearing "Jewish this" and "Jewish that." Everything became about "Jewish" and "Gentile." So now you have two classes of people. If you're not Jewish, then what are you? You're a Gentile.

The language itself created a first class and a second class citizenship. Then you start hearing words like "Noahide laws." Noahide laws were a compilation of laws that somebody put together and decided "these are the laws for the Gentiles." Believe it or not, there are Messianics who are presenting Noahide laws.

We aren't Jewish. At least I'm not, I can't speak for you. There may be some Jewish people here, but I'm not Jewish. I'm not trying to be Jewish. I'm not trying to look Jewish. I'm not trying to sound Jewish. Now, for the Jewish people; they should be Jewish, but I'm not Jewish. And we're not Seventh-Day Adventists.

The reason why I'm saying this is because at one point my own children asked:

"Are we Jewish now?"

Has anybody ever had to confront that issue within themselves?

"What are we? Are we Jewish now?"

People either confuse you with being Jewish or Seventh-Day Adventist. Has anybody ever been confused with "you're trying to be Jewish"? Let me see your hands. Nobody. Okay. What about Seventh-Day Adventist?

You see, when you start keeping the Sabbath, then you now are put into the category of being a Seventh-Day Adventist. When you start keeping the feasts, you're now put into the category of "trying to be Jewish." That is because after all, the feasts were given to the Jews, right? Wrong! You see, that's the first problem we've got. Now, notice how many of you say:

"Yeah!"

That's the first problem. We're going to address that. Now, here is where it gets complicated. If you're not Jewish-born, you're not a Gentile either, because **a Gentile is a pagan. A Gentile is an unbeliever.**

How many unbelievers have we got in the house? How many heathens are here? What about pagans? Stand up if you're a pagan. You see, this is the terminology that is associated with "Gentile." So if you're not a heathen, if you're not a pagan, if you're not an unbeliever, then you're not in the Gentile category. If you're not Jewish, you're not in the Jewish category.

> *"But wait a minute. There's only two"* [categories].

Who said that? You see, this is how we've been trained. We were trained this in the Christian Church and it is enforced and reinforced in Messianic Judaism.

The general definitions of Gentiles are pagans, heathens, nations, goy, unbeliever and non-Jew.

Speaking of me personally, I interpreted learning the Torah as learning the Jewish Scriptures. I heard several times that the Torah or Law was given to the Jews. I heard:

> *"Let the Jews interpret all of the scriptures the Jews wrote and let the Gentiles interpret all of the scriptures that the Gentiles wrote."*

How many scriptures did the Gentiles write? Now, there was one Gentile in the bunch. His name was Luke. Luke wrote the Book of *Luke* and Luke wrote the Book of *Acts*. Luke was not Hebrew. Luke was not Jewish. Luke was not a disciple of Messiah, yet Luke has a prominent place in the gospel and is responsible for giving us the *Acts* of the Apostles.

The fact is that the Torah was given to Moses to speak unto Israel. It is true however, that over time, the word of YeHoVaH has been preserved by the Jews. But the fact is that the first six books of the Bible (*Genesis, Exodus, Leviticus, Numbers,*

Deuteronomy and *Joshua*) were not written by Jews. Let me say that again. Those books were not written by Jews. It was Moses, a Levite.

If you are of the mindset that you're either Jew or Gentile, then that automatically puts all of the writers of the Old Testament and the New Testament into the "Jewish" category. I challenge all of you here today; every one of you. Go and find the word "Jew" in the first six books of the Bible. Find it.

It's not there. You see, the moment you've been given a mindset to think a certain way, then you look at the book through those lenses and automatically begin to interpret or read into things. That is *eisegesis,* not *exegesis.* The latter is where you're reading *what is actually there*. With eisegesis, you are *reading into it, something that's not even there.*

Moses was a Levite, not a Jew. He was given the oracles of YeHoVaH or the word of God. Get this. It was Moses (a Levite), not a Jew who YeHoVaH spoke with face-to-face and who spent two forty-day periods with YeHoVaH receiving these oracles.

> ***Exodus 4:14*** *– "And the anger of YeHoVaH was kindled against Moses, and he said, '**Is not Aaron the Levite your [thy] brother**?'"*

Now, if his brother is a Levite – there are other places here where we can find this. This is the one verse where we can clearly see Moses and the word "Levite" in the same verse without having to show you Moses' parents and their genealogy, but look it up for yourself. Moses was a Levite. Aaron was a Levite. Miriam was a Levite.

> *"...I know that he can speak well. And also, behold, he cometh forth to meet thee: and when he seeth thee, he will be glad in his heart."*

Joshua was not a Levite. Moses was responsible for the first five books. Joshua is responsible for the next book. Joshua was an Ephraimite of the tribe of Ephraim.

You see, when you say that all of Israel is Jewish, you put the entire tribes of Israel into one tribe. Thereby you literally *argue against scripture and YeHoVaH himself and the prophets and the Hebrew Scriptures*. It's not the Book of the Jews, but the Book of Hebrews.

The Book of *Hebrews* along with the prophet Jeremiah concerning the entire new covenant is given to the House of Judah and the House of Israel. **That's all of Israel.** The Jews are the descendants of Judah.[2] Okay? You don't believe me? See *Numbers 13:8*:

> *"from the tribe of Ephraim, Hoshea son of Nun."*

Who is "Hoshea son of Nun?" There's no Book of Hoshea.

> *"You're talking about the Book of Hosea?"*

No.

> ***Numbers 13:16*** – *"These are the names of the men Moses sent to explore the land. **(Moses gave Hoshea son of Nun the name Joshua.)**"*

This is from where we get the Book of *Joshua*. What tribe was he from? Ephraim. Ephraim became synonymous with the House of Israel.

The reason why this ministry is called the *House Of Israel* is because it encompasses all of YeHoVaH's people; not just some specific tribe.

So, to be Messianic Jewish is to be a Jew or a Jew try-to-be or wanna-be. Is there anything wrong with being Jewish? Absolutely not. There's nothing wrong with being Irish. There's nothing wrong with being African or American. Your nationality doesn't determine your relationship with the Almighty. Your obedience to the Almighty's word is what determines your

---

[2] Judah is only one of the tribes of Israel.

relationship with the Almighty regardless to what tribe, what nation, what country or what tongue you speak.

Don't let somebody put you into a second class citizenship. If you do, it's your fault. It's not theirs. A lot of these Messianic Jewish congregations (especially) do this. Listen again. Let me say that.

Samuel, the first prophet who anointed the first king of Israel, was an Ephramite. The first was an Ephramite. The first king was a Benjamite, not a Jew.

> ***1 Samuel 1:1*** *– "There was a certain man from Ramathaim, a Zuphite from the hill country of Ephraim, whose name was Elkanah son of Jeroham, the son of Elihu, the son of Tohu, the son of Zuph, an Ephraimite."*

It's this man who is the Father of Samuel, an Ephraimite. You see, if *man shall not live by bread alone but by every word that proceeds from the mouth of YeHoVaH*, we'd better take note of the words YeHoVaH used to identify his people.

As a matter of fact, the word *"Jew"* doesn't come from the mouth of YeHoVaH. It comes from *commentaries*, the commentator. The commentator is the one by whom they were first called Jews or they were first called Christians. What commentator?

> *"What? The commentator? Who is the commentator here?"*

Don't let me get "Mississippi" on you. That goes back to my roots.

Saul, the first king of Israel, was not a Jew. Saul was a Benjamite of the tribe of Benjamin. Now, I know that I'm going to get some emails:

> *"Why are you railing against the Jewish people?"*

Listen. You cannot present fact from the scripture without confronting error. It's not attacking anybody. **It is revealing what the scripture says versus what you've been taught.**

If you want to hold onto what you've been taught; let me tell you something folks. I've been knocking at this and hitting it for the longest time and I've still got people around me.

People have heard these teachings, but they are still using that same terminology, so what does that say? It says that there are some things that are deeply ingrained in our psyche and in our spirit that are difficult for us to change even when the truth is being presented. I have presented truth over and over and over and over. Instead of people embracing truth, they want to attack me for having an "issue" with the Jewish people. Do you hear what I'm saying?

Anyway, it's not going to stop me because I'm not here to preach tradition and what everybody else is saying. Even if my best friend is saying some stuff that is not right, I have a responsibility to bring correction – and I have, so don't take this as me trying to attack somebody. I have a responsibility before YeHoVaH to teach you *what his word says* regardless to what you believe or want to believe.

I know that I'm small potatoes maybe in your mind, but I know who I am in the Kingdom. I'm not afraid of any man or woman. Do you understand what I'm saying? I know who I've got to give an account to and if my standing for the truth puts me on a desert island isolated by myself – which I doubt. That's because YeHoVaH has a remnant of people who have ears to hear and they'll be right there on that island with me. We'll all be singing:

"Hosanna! Blessed be the name!"

Are you hearing me? We might be a small group, but I won't be alone.

> ***Acts 13:21*** *– "Then the people asked for a king, and he gave them Saul son of Kish,"*

Of the tribe of Judah? This is in the New Testament!

> *"...of the tribe of Benjamin, who ruled forty years."*

He's not being referred to as "Jewish." He's being referred to as a Benjamite.

You see, in the Book of *Revelation,* we know that there's not going to be one throne for one tribe. Halleluyah! There's not going to be one pillar or one gate. So we've got to dispel some notions and if you're going to hold onto the truth, you've got to let go of traditions.

It's important that people know the Biblical Facts so they are not victims to Traditions ASSUMED to be facts.

I had to go and make all of those words capitalized so that you didn't think I was trying to sneak a cuss word up in here.

Ruth – you know the one that the Book of *Ruth* is written about? Ruth was a Moabite, not a Jew.

> ***Ruth 1:22*** *– "So Naomi returned from Moab accompanied by Ruth the Moabitess, her daughter-in-law, arriving in Bethlehem as the barley harvest was beginning."*

Now that we've stated the facts of what the biblical characters' background and genealogy was, what are we? Who are we? People want to know:

> *"What do you call yourself?"*

What do we call ourselves? I'm not Jewish. I don't know if I like "Messianic." You know, Christian, Messianic Christian, Messianic Jew, Hebrew, Hebrew Israelite. What do I call myself? I'll tell you what I call myself.

I am a follower of the Son of YeHoVaH.

That's who I follow. If somebody is going to put a title on me, it's going to be me. It doesn't mean that people are not going to try to categorize you or put you into a category. I saw some people under so much pressure in their communities and schools that they decided they would take the easy way out and say:

> *"I'm Jewish."*

That's what they said.

> *"You're not Jewish. Why are you claiming to be?"*

> *"Well, if I say that I'm Jewish, then people know that I believe like the Jews believe."*

Do you really want to associate yourself with that? Let me tell you something. I disagree with myself sometimes. Can you put me into a category? Can you stereotype and say that because of my behavior that I now represent the African-Americans or the colored race? I mean, I have heard folks say:

> *"You know, you ain't colored. You ain't Black. You ain't no African-American."*

It's like, man. No matter what you call yourself, you "ain't" that. I have heard some folks who have said:

> *"You know, you're a nice Negro."*

Yeah.

> *"Wow. You speak pretty clearly for a Black guy."*

[Arthur and the audience laugh.]

You've got to have a sense of humor if you're going to live in this world. It doesn't matter. So, I am and we are followers of the Son of YeHoVaH, King of the Jews, the Prophet, the Messiah.

We are Messiahians, Messianic! Our **faith** didn't originate with the Jewish Scriptures, but with the **Hebrew Scriptures**.

Let me tell you something. **Abraham wasn't the first Hebrew**, but that's a whole other story. That's a whole other teaching. He wasn't Jewish either. As a matter of fact, *Deuteronomy 25:26* tells us that **Abraham was a Syrian; a Syrian!**

WHAT ARE THE ESSENTIALS OF OUR FAITH?

I'm glad you asked.

> *1. Faith in **YeHoVaH** and in the Messiah **Yeshua/Yehoshua** whom he sent*
>
> *2. Eating Biblically*
>
> *3. Keeping the Sabbath*
>
> *4. Keeping the Feasts*
>
> *5. Baptism of the Holy Spirit*

These are the essentials of our faith.

Now, you'll notice that I have YeHoVaH bold and underlined. I have Yeshua/Yehoshua bold and underlined. The reason why they're bold and underlined is because one of the biggest issues that seems to separate believers in Messiah is "the name." There are a lot of names out there that people are ready to fight and die over. You know?

> *"His name is not YeHoVaH. It's Yahweh."*
>
> *"His name is not Yahweh. It's Yehua."*
>
> *"His name is not Yehua. It's Yehowah."*
>
> *"His name is not Yehowah. It's Yahveh."*
>
> *"His name is not Yahveh. It's Yehuvah."*
>
> *"His name is not Yehuvah. It's Ehyeh Asher Ehyeh."*

The list just goes on and on and on and on. People fight and separate and split [over this]. The truth of the matter is that we have to depend upon the tools that we have been given to try to come as close to what the name is as we possibly can.

I don't claim to be an ancient Hebrew scholar. I have tools that I use to research. Based on those tools that I use to research, I have to acknowledge that all of these tools that have been given to me to do the research with have been given to me by people who have done the research. So in a sense I am (to a degree) at the mercy of those who have given us the tools. Do you understand what I'm saying?

The *Strong's Concordance* is a tool that most people use. Some people go into other tools when dealing with words that are deeper than the Strong's Concordance. But even those who go deeper than the Strong's Concordance use the Strong's Concordance as a basis because they're all using the same numbering system. This numbering system is geared toward the King James Bible.

There are others who have come up with additional tools that we have to trust. In essence we have to trust that the tools we've been given are the right tools. We have to trust that because I wasn't there when Moses asked him what his name was and he heard what he said. I wasn't there.

I now have to resolve in myself what it is that I believe based on the evidence and research that I have searched out for myself. Once I've searched that research out, I can now present it and say:

"This is why I believe what I believe."

It's not based on what somebody else said. It's not based on somebody else's research although I had to use tools that were given to me by these expert researchers. I have charts. I have letters. I have signs. I have the Paleo-Hebrew alphabet, the ancient Hebrew alphabet.

You see, people think they hear Hebrew. They don't realize sometimes that there is ancient Hebrew. There is Classical Hebrew. There is Biblical Hebrew. There is Modern Hebrew. There is Israeli Hebrew. So when you begin to talk about Hebrew, which Hebrew are you talking about?

"Well, in the Hebrew..."

What Hebrew? First let's establish which Hebrew you're using. Do you understand what I'm saying? You see, I'm not assuming that you're using the right Hebrew to tell me what "that" means in the Hebrew, so let's establish which Hebrew you are using. That's important.

When you go from country to country and even in some cases from neighborhood to neighborhood; you're going to find that people are saying words that you think mean one thing, but they mean something totally different.

Here are the essentials again:

1. Faith in YeHoVaH and in Messiah Yeshua

2. Eating Biblically

3. Keeping the Sabbath

4. Keeping the Feasts

5. The Baptism of the Holy Spirit

Interestingly enough, all five of these particular doctrines are in the first three books of the Bible.

We know that in the beginning is the nameless one called "God." We know that in the beginning when the Earth was formed or void, there is the Holy Spirit. We know that signs and seasons in the first book of the Bible deal with and are translated as feasts and festivals. He gives us the feasts. He gives us the festivals. At the end of his creation and what capped creation off and without which creation would not be complete is the Sabbath.

So, you've got these instructions.

> *"Here's what you're going to eat. This is food for you: that which is bearing seed. I have given you the trees and the plants."*

YeHoVaH deals with food. He deals with the Sabbath. He deals with the feasts. He deals with the Holy Spirit and he deals with presenting himself to his creation all in the first three chapters of *Genesis*.

You've got to search it to find it. Some of it is obvious:

> *"In the beginning, God..."*

Okay, we found the Father.

> *"The Holy Spirit was hovering over the deep."*

Do you see?

> *"...seed-bearing plants."*

That's food for you, you see.

Faith in YeHoVaH and in Messiah – this is critical. Christians want to teach you that faith came through Jesus Christ and that the law came through Moses, but grace and truth came through Jesus. Well, if faith in Jesus is in fact true (and it is), in the beginning was the word and the word was God and the word "Jesus" became flesh and dwelled among us.

When was he? He was in the beginning, so let's roll with that. Do you want to say: "faith came through Jesus"? Well, okay. He was with the Almighty in the beginning, if that's what you call it, okay? Can you agree with that? If you can't, let's just rip *John* right out of the New Testament. Just take it out. *Revelation* 12. Let's go to the end of the book.

> ***Revelation 12:17*** *– "And the dragon was wroth with the woman, and went to make war with the remnant of her seed, which keep the*

commandments of God, and have the testimony of Yeshua Messiah [Christ Jesus]."

So here we have it. **They keep the commandments and they have faith in Yeshua,** not one or the other. He's not talking about Jews and Christians. He's talking about the seed of the woman – the seed of the woman that's going to crush something's head up in here.

Revelation 14:12 *– "Here is the patience of the saints..."*

Just in case you didn't fit in the other category.

"...the saints: here are they that keep the commandments of God, and the faith of Yeshua."

That's for you end times prophets. **Faith is a gift given to us by YeHoVaH (God) to believe in him.** You can't believe in him without this gift. Where did it come from? It came from him. Why? Because he wants to be believable!

The reason why you say that you are a believer is because the Almighty who created the Heavens and the Earth gave you the ability to believe.

For those who do not believe in the creator, guess what? You don't have a mind, so your wisdom is foolish. After all, that's what the scriptures teach. It's not Bailey.

Romans 12:3 *– "For I say, through the grace given unto me, to every man that is among you, not to think of himself more highly than he ought to think; but to think soberly, according as God has dealt..."*

To some men?

"..to every man the measure of faith."

No, it is to every man on the planet whether believer, non-believer, pagan or heathen. Every person out there has the capability and ability to believe. Whether they believe in the Almighty or not, they believe in something. And their ability to believe is a gift of YeHoVaH, because he's given it to every man.

> ***Ephesians 2:8*** – *"For by grace are ye saved through faith; and that not of yourselves: it is the gift..."*

This is a favorite verse for Christians.

> *"Aw brother, it's by grace that we are saved."*

It's not grace by itself. It's *grace through faith.* Faith in what? Faith in whom? Faith in Yeshua? Faith in Jesus? You see, Yeshua came to reconcile man to his creator. That's why he says:

> *"When you pray, pray this prayer: 'Our Father who are in heaven...'"*

Where was Yeshua when he told them this? He was right there on Earth with them. He didn't say:

> *"Pray to me."*

For some reason, Christians got the wrong memo.

> *"Lord Jesus...we come to you in the name of Jesus...asking you Jesus...Father God..."*

Again, I'm not trying to make fun of anybody, but if you sometimes just pay attention to what people say, people will tell you and reveal their confusion. Many people are confused. Why? It's because religion confuses people. It gives you a religion that is a counterfeit to *faith in the word* (which is true).

Once a person has been given the counterfeit, they don't know how to differentiate. The counterfeit to them is real. The counterfeit is real. The main way to identify a counterfeit is that you have to know what the real looks like.

Now [with money] they've got the pens. The pens used to work until counterfeiters got smarter. They started bleaching five dollar bills and reprinting them as twenties, as fifties and as hundred dollar bills. The pen is designed to see if the paper is real; not the bill. It's not for the denomination. It's for the paper. So when the pen hits the paper, the paper is real even though the bill is a counterfeit. The pen is useless.

Then they've got these little lights in the banks. They put the bills under the light. The only way you can really tell the difference between a counterfeit bill and a real bill is that you have to hold it to the light because there are markings that you can't counterfeit. You can't counterfeit them and you'll see.

With foreigners, it is different. You won't see a whole lot of Americans doing this. If you give an American a one hundred dollar bill, oftentimes they've got to pull out their pen or they've got to get their little light. But most foreigners; if you do business with foreigners, they'll look at it.

"Okay. Okay. Okay."

[Arthur snaps his fingers.] They see it right away. Now, it's something when you look at the bill and you've got a hundred dollar bill with Jefferson's picture. It's like:

> *"Wait a minute. Jefferson ain't on no hundred dollar bill. How come his picture is in the paper, but Franklin is on the bill? Something's not right."*

You've got one face here and another face there. That's a counterfeit "bro." The pen is not going to tell you that. And guess what? If you take a counterfeit to the bank, you didn't counterfeit it, but you've got it. Guess who's going to lose?

You see, there are a whole lot of folks who are going to show up on Judgment Day with counterfeit faith. They've got the counterfeit. They've got religion. They've got the *form* of Godliness.

It is a gift. Adam and Eve had faith, but they used it to rebel by believing something other than what God had said. This is exactly what people do when they have their counterfeit religion and you show them what "thus saith YeHoVaH." **They hold onto their denominational doctrine even though what YeHoVaH says in his word contradicts their faith.**

That was Adam and Eve's problem. YeHoVaH said one thing. "Reverend Satan" came along. Yeah, I said "Reverend Satan" or "Bishop" or "Apostle Satan."

> *"Well, did God really say that? You know, what God literally meant was..."*

Now they want to get literal on you.

> *"But that word 'literally' means..."*

> *"Well, come on..."*

Cain had faith, but he used it to rebel by believing something other than what YeHoVaH said. YeHoVaH says:

> *"Cain, why is your face wroth? Why are you looking like that? Don't you know that if you do well, you will be accepted too? But sin is crouching at your door. Its desire is to have you."*

Let me tell you something folks. Don't you think for a moment that sin is not crouching at your door. It's crouching every moment you get up. It's crouching in the morning, in the noonday and in the midnight hour. Yes it is, and its desire is to just give you a little taste; just a "tee-nightchy" bit. You know? You see, Satan knows that all it takes is just a little taste. That's all. It doesn't take a whole lot.

> *"You don't have to...just taste it! Come on, just taste it!"*

See? Once you get to taste:

> *"Mmm that's good! Can I get some more?"*

Next thing you know, "pfew!" He's got you – a little leaven. In order for you to hold onto and maintain your faith, you're going to have to stand upon truth in the midst of a perverted and ungodly generation that's simply trying to get you to taste it.

> *"Just taste a little bit. Surely God is not going to hold it against you. I mean, after all, God made it."*
>
> *"Yeah, he did, didn't he?"*

Now, I didn't see him out there harvesting it. I didn't see him manufacturing and putting his little cut on it trying to get you hooked.

> *"Here. Just taste it. Don't worry about it. Don't worry about it."*

That's the way the drug dealers work. That's the way Satan works.

> *"Just taste a little. Here. Try this. Try this. If you like it, come back and see me."*

Next thing you know, you find people who have tried it. Now they have given the shirt off their back. They're giving them their bodies.

I watched a commercial the other day. This person came into the store to buy a cigarette. Have you seen that commercial? And they didn't have enough money? The store owner looked at her and said:

> *"You don't have enough money. It's going to cost you a little bit more than this."*

The person stood there and then just grabs some skin. [Arthur makes a ripping sound.] She ripped it off of her face and put it onto the counter. The idea is that cigarette smoke and all of this stuff that you're doing is killing you. It's defiling the temple of YeHoVaH. And at the same time it's like:

> *"Why do you...?"*

You know, after seventeen years of smoking and looking back at myself and looking at others; I don't know why I couldn't see myself the way I see people today. The only explanation that I have is that I had blinders on. I was blind though I claimed to be able to see.

Human beings blowing smoke – it really doesn't even make sense, yet all it took was one hit and another and pretty soon instead of going to get cigarettes, the cigarettes got you. It's the same with alcohol and drugs and other stuff. That's why I say to a virgin:

> *"You need to keep your virginity as long as you can, because if you mess around and let your virginity go before it's time, you are up a creek without a paddle."*

For those of you who have lost it, you know what I'm talking about. For those of you who haven't, the pressure is on to give it up. There's a lot of pressure on our young people.

"What do you mean you're still a virgin?"

Now being a virgin is like anathema. It's like a curse.

"A virgin?"

"Yes, I'm a virgin and the reason why I'm a virgin is because I don't want to be as confused as you are."

Do you remember who you gave your virginity to? What did they do with it? Where is it at now? Where is your virginity? It's gone and some of you can't even remember when it left.

"It's been so long ago."

And that's precious. You're going to see that being a true believer means holding onto your virginity. The world is trying to get you to give it up; not YeHoVaH. The world wants you to be like it. The world wants you to be like one of them. They want you to be sad and miserable and confused.

> *"Oh, now you're one of us. You ain't no virgin no more. Ha ha ha!"*

That's sad, isn't it? We've allowed the world to minimize the things of YeHoVaH to such a degree to where the things that YeHoVaH calls "sacred" are no longer sacred. **Your virginity is sacred!** Don't let anybody tell you anything different, because once you lose it, it's gone and you can't get it back!

Abel was *the first to use faith* to please YeHoVaH. He died because of it. I wonder if that's a message there. **You see, when you use your faith to please YeHoVaH, your own family might turn on you.**

> ***Hebrews 11:1*** *– "Now faith is the substance of things hoped for, the evidence of things not seen. ²For by it the elders obtained a good report. ³Through faith we understand that the worlds were framed by the word of YeHoVaH, so that things which are seen were not made of things which do appear. ⁴By faith Abel..."*

Abel is the first person in the Bible besides YeHoVaH. Get this.

Through faith we understand that the worlds were framed by YeHoVaH's word. YeHoVaH exercised faith. He gave Adam faith. He gave Missus Adam faith. He gave Cain faith, Abel faith and Seth faith. Satan's got faith too. Believe it or not, he believes.

> *"Do you believe? Ha ha ha!"*

Even the devil believes and trembles because he knows that the way he used his faith is going to cost him some splish-splash and taking a serious bath in the Lake of Fire along with those who like to hang out with him.

> *"Party over there. It ain't over here."*

Some of you all will get that [joke] next week.

We see that YeHoVaH exercised faith. When Abel exercised faith, I could see Father now was like:

> *"All right, he has redeemed his Momma and his Daddy."*

> **Hebrews 11:4**, *"By faith Abel offered unto God a more excellent sacrifice than Cain, by which he obtained witness that he was righteous..."*

He obtained witness that he was righteous by giving the offering that was a sacrifice. I'm not talking about "no" sacrifice of praise because most people's sacrifice of praise "ain't no" sacrifice.

"Oh, give the Lord a sacrifice of praise!"

Let me catch you when you're at your down moment. *Now* praise him. Praise him *now*! *Now* it's a sacrifice. You're going through? You're at the bottom? You're ready to throw in the towel?

> *"Oh boy, we've got a sacrifice of praise moment now. Come on! Give him a sacrifice of praise!"*

> *"Better get out of my face! You're about to get hurt up in here. Don't feel like praising. Don't mess with me. Don't let me go 'carnal' on you or let me lose my salvation."*

> *"Yeah. You already lost it."*

Let everything that has breath praise him. Are you breathing? [Arthur laughs.]

> *"...by which he obtained witness that he was righteous, God testifying of his gifts: and by it he being dead yet he speaks."*

God gave man faith to be able to please him. The very nature of faith is the ability to believe in that which is unseen. When we trust in YeHoVaH for that which is yet unseen or not manifested, he causes it to manifest or to become visible.

You don't need faith to obtain that which you already have. **Without faith it is impossible to please God.** You see, Father wants you to please him. That's why he gave us faith. He says:

> **Hebrews 11:6** – *"But without faith it is impossible to please him: for he that cometh to God must believe that he is, and that he is a rewarder of them that diligently seek him."*

You see, he wants you to please him. He knows that without the gift of faith, you can't. That's why he gave it. He says:

> *"You can please me. You can please me, but in order for you to please me, you've got to be willing to let go of you!"*

It's the only way.

We're talking about *Messianic 101*. Every man has been given a measure of faith. Faith can be used to your benefit or you can use faith to your demise. Faith is a system of belief.

What do you believe? You see, what you believe is what you say. What is coming out of your mouth is what is formulating in your heart. Out of the abundance of the heart is what the mouth says. So, all I've got to do is listen to what you say and I can tell you what you believe. You see, your mouth doesn't lie when it comes down to faith.

You can say you believe, but now do you have the corresponding actions? When you speak with your mouth – well, let me rephrase that. Your mouth *can* lie. Faith coming out of your mouth is going to be accompanied by action. *Words without action or faith without works is dead.* If you say that you believe something, then I should see it. I should see that in your walk.

This is how you're going to know the counterfeit Christian or you're going to know the counterfeit Messianic or you're going to know the counterfeit Messiahian. Those who claim to be a part of us who aren't; all you've got to do is listen to them.

Just listen. They'll tell you what's in them, but when they want something, they'll tell you what they think you want to hear.

You've got to be able to distinguish what you want to hear from what people are saying and what they are consistent in. You see, people will tell you where they are. They'll tell you what they believe. And if they tell you who they are and what they believe, why is it so hard for you to believe?

"Oh! I'm shocked!"

"Why are you shocked?"

"I can't believe she did that."

"Why can't you?"

You see, you catch people in the act who have told you over and over what they are about.

Prior to the giving of the Holy Spirit in *Acts*, those who practiced the religion of the Jews only knew one way for non-Jewish people to come to (their) God. You see, the God of Abraham, Isaac and Jacob belonged to the Hebrew people. Now, this may come as a shock for some people, but Ishmael was Hebrew.

Many of the people that are called Muslims are Semitic Hebrews. You see, the moment people want to identify Muslims to Ishmael; Ishmael was a son of Abraham. How can Abraham be a Hebrew and Ishmael not?

Oh yeah. We're attacking mindsets and every high thing that exalts itself against the knowledge of YeHoVaH, the God of Abraham, Isaac and Ya'kov (or Avraham, Yitzhak or however you want to pronounce it). **The God of Abraham was also the God of Ishmael.**

As believers were coming to faith in Messiah, several issues arose, but the one that got the most attention was the issue that arose in *Acts* 15. The issue that arose in *Acts* 6 concerning the Grecian widows and the Hebrew-speaking widows dealt with how they were being treated in the daily rations. But the big issue came up in *Acts* 15 when these individuals had to deal with non-Hebrew people coming into the faith and calling on the name of the God of Abraham, Isaac and Jacob.

"What do we do with these Gentiles?"

Much of that is in these teachings here. [Arthur holds up DVD teachings available at www.ArthurBaileyMinistries.com.]

Acts 15: The First Jerusalem Council

Keeping Torah Living Spirit-Filled

The New Covenant

We have all of these teachings. We don't make a big deal out of them, but I'm going to tell you. They are full of information that if you avail yourself to; you will find that a lot of the stuff that we've just taken to believe, we can dispute a lot of it from the Bible.

This issue in *Acts* 15 was a very serious issue. Every last one of us faced this issue whether we accept it or not. If you were brought up in a Jewish home, you were brought up in Messianic Judaism. You see, Messianic Judaism to the Orthodox Jew who rejects Yeshua is a Jew who is religious and who is looking for the Messiah. They are *Messianic* Jews. Why? Because they are looking for the Messiah.

Modern Gentiles identify Messianic Jews as Jews who believe in Messiah – the Messiah who has already come. *Messianic Jews are Jews who believe in the Messiah who is going to come.* You see, the terminology is the same. It just depends on which side of this Messianic Jew you are on. You could be having the same conversation, but be talking about two different things.

This person claims to be Messianic Jewish (who's looking). This person claims to be Messianic Jew (who believes in the Messiah who has already come). This one believes that he is yet to come, but has not come. Unless you define the conversation, it is unclear. This is how a lot of folks who come out of the Gentile Christian Church come into Messianic Judaism. They're given these books. The next thing you know, they're in a synagogue looking for the Messiah to come. They've denied the faith. They've denied that Yeshua has come in the flesh. They've walked away.

Now, *that's* a person who has "fallen from grace" because they came into the faith believing in Messiah and they were given Messianic Jewish material. They wanted to learn Hebrew. They wanted to immerse themself in the culture. They found themself in a Jewish synagogue, davening and praying to the East. The next thing you know, they're looking for the Messiah to come like he hasn't already come.

That's the *real issue* that's going on right here in *Acts* 15. This issue brought all of the apostles and elders into one place to have a very serious discussion about what to do with the Gentiles that were coming to faith in Messiah Yeshua.

You have to understand ladies and gentlemen, that these individuals already met the criteria of a believer. The individuals that *Acts* 15 have gathered about, is because of this issue. If you begin in verse 1, you'll find that some brothers came down from Jerusalem and began to teach.

> ***Acts 15:1*** *– "And certain men which came down from Judaea taught the brethren, and said, 'Except ye be circumcised after the manner of Moses, ye cannot be saved.'"*

Let me just break this down in a nutshell because we're dealing with a culture [then] that is very different than the culture that we're dealing with [today]. The only way for a person who was not Jewish to come into the Hebrew faith was that they had to *convert to Judaism*. *Acts* 2 calls these individuals "proselytes." They've converted to Judaism.

[They would teach that] the only way you can come into faith in YeHoVaH is that you convert to Judaism. They were teaching that since Yeshua came from YeHoVaH, then you now had to convert to Judaism before you could believe and accept the Jewish Messiah.

"He is our Messiah. He is a Jewish Messiah."

He's not a Gentile Messiah. He is a Jewish Messiah and in order for you to accept the Jewish Messiah, you have to become Jewish. That's the issue here. It's about *conversion*. You see, hundreds of years; all the way back to Simeon and Jacob, when Simeon said:

"Do you want to marry my sister? You've got to become one of us. You've got to be circumcised."

CIRCUMCISION THROUGH ABRAHAM

The key in this verse is that *Moses did not give a manner of circumcision.* **Circumcision came through Abraham.** Ishmael was circumcised. I keep hitting that point because people hear Ishmael and they think:

"Oh tear us!"

Well you know, I hope the congregations don't go and do further. That's my prayer. It's like:

"Father...You know, you keep bringing these messages and folks like a nice packaged Messianic Jewish Hebrew Roots type of message that makes them feel all warm and fuzzy inside. It makes you want to just go out and send some money to Israel."

He said:

"Except ye be circumcised after the manner of Moses, ye cannot be saved."

What are they doing? They're associating salvation to circumcision. Do you see this? They're associating salvation to circumcision.

You do not have to be circumcised to be saved!

YeHoVaH saved and delivered Israel out of Egypt before he gave them the law. Yes he did. **We don't keep the law to be saved. We keep the commandments of YeHoVaH because he has brought us into his Kingdom and a kingdom without law is chaos.**

Imagine a city without law. There was a movie where they decided to rescind the law. I didn't see the movie, so I have no idea, but I read the review or something like that. It was:

"No laws for a year."

Or something like that. So whoever you want dead; you can do whatever you want and you won't go to jail. Imagine if they were to do that today. Some of us – I'm sure you can probably think of some folks.

"No brother, not me. I'm a...what am I?"

You're a follower of Messiah.

To recap:

1. Faith in YeHoVaH

They already had his.

2. Eating Biblically

They already did this.

3. Baptism of the Holy Spirit

They already had this.

4. Keeping the Sabbath

They already did it.

5. Keeping the Feasts

It is already part of the culture.

In *Acts* 15 as Gentiles were coming to the faith; you have to ask. How are they coming? How did they know? Faith comes by what? It comes by hearing. The message of faith had been preached to them and they responded to the message of faith. Now they're coming out of their cultures. It's like somebody said:

> *"Wait a minute. We can't have this. Hold it, hold it, hold it, hold it! That's not how we've done it! That's not how it's been done for years and years and centuries! That's not how my Daddy did it! That's not how my Granddaddy did it! That's not how the patriarchs did it! If you want to come to the faith that we have, you've got to come according to the way all Gentiles come! You've got to be circumcised!"*

That's the issue. Let me just give you this because it became really simple that the real issue is this.

> ***Acts 15:20*** *– "...abstain[ing] from pollution of idols, and from fornication."*

The church just got that part. It's:

> *"Just abstain from fornication. You don't want to keep the law. Just abstain from fornication, from things strangled, and from blood."*

Now the church rejects the law.

This is the word that was given to the people who were coming into faith in Messiah and who weren't Jews. He says:

> *"You've got to do this stuff. If you do this you'll be fine."*

What if you don't?

PART TWO: WE ARE DISCIPLERS

I started to do this teaching because more and more people's eyes are being opened to the faith once delivered to the saints. New believers are being added to the family of YeHoVaH on a regular basis. As I said previously, it is important that they get started on the right way. As believers who have been on this way, we have a responsibility to new believers to be a disciple, a mentor and a coach. **We have to be a discipler.**

You might say:

> *"Well, I don't know how to do that. I don't feel comfortable doing that."*

Listen. If you know this much [Arthur holds fingers pinched together indicating a small amount], you can teach that much. You see, there is so much that is in you that you don't even know is there until you are put in a position and it is drawn out.

You will find yourself being amazed. That's because if you've been around here for any length of time, the words that are spoken in this place are Spirit. We speak by the Spirit of YeHoVaH. Those words (which are Spirit) go into your spirit. There are many things that are being said in this ministry that bypass your ears and that go straight into your spirit.

Now it is residing within you waiting and dormant until some unsuspecting "victim" comes along and challenges you in a specific way. The Bible says that the Almighty raises up this standard. Out of nowhere the word just raises itself. You will find things coming out of your mouth and it will be like:

> *"Wow. Where did that come from?"*

I know where it came from. It came from your spirit because you are being equipped. The only way you are going to be able to maximize what you have been taught is by teaching it and by sharing it. You have to put yourself out there.

> *"I'm learning so that I can teach."*

That's the mindset that you have to have. It's not:

> *"I'm learning so that I can know."*

It's:

> *"I'm learning so that I can teach."*

The way I know what I am to teach is what I have applied in my life and what I see the Almighty manifesting himself in. It's not just about getting information and passing it on. It's about receiving that word, applying that word and seeing the Almighty backing his word up. Now I'm confident in the word that I've received and I can pass that on.

Sometimes people say:

> *"You know, you talk about yourself a lot."*

Well, the only things I can talk about are my experiences. I can't talk about your experiences. Do you know what I'm saying? I can't talk about your experiences. I can only talk about what the Father has done in me and I can talk about that with confidence. As one of my mentors once said:

> *"A man with an experience is not at the mercy of someone with a teaching."*

If you have experienced healing in your life and somebody comes along and says:

> *"God doesn't heal."*

It's like:

> *"Really? He doesn't? Then what happened to me? Are you saying that I wasn't healed when I was there? Were you there? I know that I was blind, but now I see."*

We have to be disciplers. We have to be mentors. We have to be coaches. We have to find someone that we can minister to.

The reason why I'm standing here for three solid years Sabbath after Sabbath, feast after feast, Thursday after Thursday and in Discipleship and Leadership is because I have somebody to teach. Do you hear what I'm saying? I can't go A.W.O.L.![3]

When you have people that you can teach, I'm telling you. They draw stuff out of you. There are people who ask me questions that I don't have the answers to and it sends me on a search. If they didn't ask questions and if I didn't have answers, I probably wouldn't search. You need people to pull out of you what the Father has put in you. You would be amazed at what has been deposited in you.

New believers to the faith have a lot of questions. They don't want to mess it up. They want to do things the right way. Unfortunately there are too many who are teaching new believers the traditions of men instead of the true Gospel of the Kingdom.

Today there is as much confusion surrounding being Messianic as there is in denominational Christianity. We are going to clear up a lot of that confusion and help people who are coming into the faith get started on the right track. Again, this message is not an attack on anyone, but because of the content, it may appear that way. I'm not trying to attack anyone. I'm not trying to speak negative or evil about anyone.

As another one of my mentors said:

"Teach what you believe, not what you don't."

I'm not here to teach what I don't believe. I'm not here to question what somebody else is teaching. I'm not here to challenge somebody else's teaching and give a response to a message that I heard last week and spend the rest of the service

---

[3] A.W.O.L. is a military term meaning "absent without leave" (or permission to leave with possibly no intent on returning).

teaching against something I heard. That's not what I'm here for. I'm here to teach what I know.

We have to stick to facts, not traditions. Too many people prefer traditions over facts even when the scriptural facts are presented in a clear and concise way. One of the things that we do here is try to do things really simply.

What are the Essentials of Our Faith?

*1. Faith in **YeHoVaH** and in the Messiah **Yeshua/Yehoshua** whom he sent.*

It is important that this faith is in the Messiah that he sent. You see, there are people who have faith in YeHoVaH. There are people who call upon the name of YeHoVaH and Yahweh and Yehouah. There are people who are so into getting the right name that they ignore the Messiah whom he sent.

If we or they or any person reject the Messiah, they are not of him. It's important that you understand that. If I stand up here and say to you:

"I do not believe that Yeshua is the Messiah."

There's a problem! The Bible says that we are not even to bid such a one "Godspeed" and yet because of so much confusion, not only are people bidding them "Godspeed," but they are supporting the ministries! That's how much confusion is out there right now.

2. Eating Biblically

It's New Testament.

3. Keeping the Sabbath

It's New Testament.

4. Keeping the Feasts

It's New Testament and certainly [so is]:

5. Baptism of the Holy Spirit

You can be in Messianic congregations and have been in Messianic congregations for a number of years and not see anybody get healed. You don't see anybody get delivered. Folks are smoking and getting drunk and having multiple wives. That's because they want to gravitate to certain *portions of the Torah* while rejecting the message of Messiah.

Not here. In *Acts* 15 as Gentiles were coming to the faith, one must ask:

"How are they coming?"

"How did they know to come to the faith in the Messiah?"

Well, that's a pretty easy one. They were instructed. In *Acts 15:20*, we know. This is getting ahead of *Acts 15:1*, which we are going to look at here in just a moment.

When the Jerusalem Council came together, they came together because Gentiles (non-Hebrews) were coming to the faith in Messiah. There were people. It's almost like this. I guess if I was to get really "out there" – I think I can get really out there. Imagine the prostitutes in Charlotte, North Carolina giving their heart to Yeshua and the next day showing up here straight from the street. Imagine what that would look like and what our response to it would be; especially if they showed up in their work clothes.

You see, its' a shock. It's like:

"Who—ahhhhh!"

You know? Because we don't have lap cloths and other types of things, you have to ask yourself:

"How would you respond to that?"

There are all kinds of things that go against our belief that we have to respond to. It's one thing as long as it stays "out there." It's another thing when it walks into our space. Now we have to deal with it. Married women are watching their husbands.

> *"What are you looking at? Don't look in that direction!"*

[Arthur laughs.]

You know, brothers will bow! They put blinders on [holds his hands on either side of his eyes.]

> *"I'm just going to look down at my Bible. I'm not looking up. I'm just going to look down; just look down."*

[Arthur humorously bends way down.]

You have to ask yourself.

> *"How would you respond?"*

I mean, that's going to the extreme, but here it is that you have people in a culture who have been taught all of their lives that those Gentiles eat rats. They eat cats. They eat dogs. They eat abominable things, detestable things. They are uncircumcised and we're to have nothing to do with them. Now they show up in your fellowship.

> *"Who-uhhh!! Who let those Gentiles in here?!"*

Now you've got to deal with it. This is the issue that these individuals are facing. It's a religious issue. It's a spiritual issue. But it is also a doctrinal issue that now has to be addressed. That is because basically it is about what you've been taught. And if you have been taught a certain way to be "right," then everybody else is "wrong."

So the disciples came together. The apostles came together. They decided, based on the Holy Spirit's leading, that:

> ***Acts 15:20*** *– "But that we write unto them, that they abstain from pollutions of idols, and from*

fornication, and from things strangled, and from blood."

Acts 15:21 *– "For Moses of old time hath in every city them that preach him, being read in the synagogues every Sabbath day."*

We looked at this earlier, but we didn't expound on it. I want us to go back to verse 1.

Acts 15:1 *– "And certain men which came down from Judaea **taught the brethren,**'"*

They taught the brethren.

"...and said, 'Except ye be circumcised after the manner of Moses, ye cannot be saved.'"

Here is what's going on. Somehow someone decided that they were going to do a circumcision check in the congregation. They identified that typically they don't really have to do a circumcision check in there because Gentiles don't get circumcised. So if they are Gentiles, chances are they are uncircumcised brutes and how can these uncircumcised Gentiles claim faith in Yeshua? So it was:

"You're not saved! You're not saved unless you have been circumcised."

"But wait a minute. We're filled with the Spirit. We've been baptized in water [probably]. We have the gifts operating in us. So you are saying that because we haven't been circumcised, we can't be saved?"

As if circumcision comes before salvation. There's another group out there [today] who says:

"If you don't speak in tongues, you're not saved!"

"Now wait a minute. I've had the power of the Almighty rest upon me. I prayed. My

> *relationship with him is in good standing. I know it because I hear his voice. I've laid hands on sick people. They've gotten well. He's given me words of knowledge, words of wisdom. I've spoken these things to people and you're going to tell me now that if I don't speak in tongues, I'm not saved? Oh!!"*

Unfortunately too many people who have had the manifestation of the presence of the Almighty manifesting in their lives and who have never spoken in tongues hear these words and their faith is affected. That's what is going on here.

These individuals' faith is being affected by someone who is preaching something that they ought not to be preaching. We are going to find out that they were never sent. They went. There's a difference between people who just went, from those who have been sent.

Right now in our nation and around the world, there are people who just "went." They are prognosticating doom and gloom and end times and the Jubilee. They are snaring and shipwrecking people. It is just like on the Day of Pentecost.

"What shall we do? What must we do?"

You see, when people come into your life and shipwreck your faith, you look to them for answers. Now they have you just where they want you — looking to them. Why does this stuff keep selling? It's because people keep buying it. It doesn't matter how many people came and said:

> *"The end of the world is near. It's going to happen on this date. It's going to happen on this date."*

> *"No, it's going to happen on that date."*

Those dates go and come. Some more come. Those dates come and go. Some more dates come. There are people right now predicting dates.

The word here, "brethren" is the word: "*adelfos*" meaning: (as a connective participle) and "from the womb"; a brother (literal or figurative) near or remote [much like **Hebrew** word]: – brother.

Basically what they are saying is:

> ***Acts 15:1*** *– "And certain men which came down from Judaea **taught the brethren**, and said, 'Except ye be circumcised after the manner of Moses, ye cannot be saved.'"*

These were individuals who were part of the House of YeHoVaH. They were brothers already and who were being taught that except they were circumcised, they can't be saved.

KEEPING THE SABBATH

Yeshua taught by what he did and by what he taught. We're going to touch more on this because in *Acts 15*, a lot of these issues are addressed. Again, what are the essentials? They are:

> *1. Faith in **YeHoVaH** and in the Messiah **Yeshua/Yehoshua** whom he sent*

We dealt with that in the last section.

> *2. Eating Biblically*

> *3. Keeping the Sabbath*

> *4. Keeping the Feasts*

> *5. Baptism of the Holy Spirit*

Notice that I didn't say eating "kosher." I said <u>eating biblically</u>. There is a difference between eating biblically and eating kosher. To eat kosher means that you have to submit yourself to some Jewish standards. I kind of avoid the term "kosher" because the term "kosher" is associated with a particular group of people and to eat kosher means that you have to eat like they eat. But there are some things that they eat that they call kosher that are not biblical.

The first thing we see in verse number 1 is that they are brethren. In order for them to be brethren, they must be part of the same family. In order for them to be part of the same family, they have received Yeshua. In order for them to have received Yeshua, they have heard the message of faith.

FAITH COMES BY HEARING

Faith comes by hearing and hearing by the word. They are already people of faith and their faith is in Yeshua and thus [they are] the brethren. Yeshua taught by what he did and by what he said.

> ***Acts 1:1*** – *'The former treatise have I made, O Theophilus, of all that Yeshua began both to do and teach,"*
>
> ***Acts 1:2*** – *"Until the day in which he was taken up, after that he through the Holy Spirit had given commandments unto the apostles whom he had chosen:"*

Yeshua taught that the things that he did, we shall do. So he is saying:

> *"Listen. There are some things that I'm going to tell you and there are some things that I'm going to show you. Now, the things that you see me do, you do. I'm telling you right now that the things that I do, you shall do."*

When the disciples didn't understand something, they asked questions. One of the things they had a challenge with was this. Here is one thing that Yeshua did that is important. I mean, all of this is important. When Yeshua prayed, he went to a private place to pray. He typically left them at a distance. So he's over there praying and they're over there watching him pray, but not knowing how he prayed. Here's one thing that he did that they didn't hear, so they said:

> "Do you know what? I wonder how he prayed?"

They heard John. John taught his disciples how to pray.

> "Maybe we should ask him to teach us how to pray."

The reason why they were asking him how they were to pray was probably because they didn't know how to pray and because they weren't there alongside of him praying when he prayed. They weren't hearing him pray and the words that he was using to pray with. He says to them:

> "When you pray, pray **after this manner**."

It was not:

> "Pray this prayer."

So people learn the Lord's Prayer::

> "Our Father, who are in Heaven, hallowed be thy name..."

That's the prayer they pray. But he is saying:

> "Listen. You pray after this manner. Your Father is your Father. You don't have to have a script to talk to him by."

The Lord's Prayer is a script. You don't need a script. All you need is a heart to pray and to share with him what's going on in you. Now, when you don't know how to pray what you're feeling, your spirit knows exactly what you're feeling and it can communicate with the Spirit of YeHoVaH in a language that you don't even know. It's called tongues and more specifically, *unknown tongues*.

Why are they unknown tongues? It's because you don't know them. Your spirit is praying and you don't even understand what your spirit is praying because your spirit is fruitful but your mind is not. Your brain is not. Thus you tap into the Spirit and say to the Spirit:

> *"My spirit is praying. I don't understand what my spirit is praying. Please interpret what my spirit is saying to you."*

Now you have the interpretation of tongues; especially if you are going to speak in tongues in a public congregational setting. That's a work of the Holy Spirit.

> ***John 14:11*** *– "Believe me that I am in the Father, and the Father in me: or else believe me for the very works' sake."*
>
> ***John 14:12*** *– "Verily, verily, I say unto you, He that believeth on me, the works that I do shall he do also; and greater works than these shall he do; because I go unto my Father."*

Now, this goes into everything Yeshua did. He says:

> *"What I do, you're going to do."*

When he says:

> *"Follow me."*

He is saying:

> *"I want you to see how I live. I want you to see what I do. I want you to see how I address certain situations. I want you to see how I deal with certain conflicts. I want you to see everything that I do because I am discipling you."*

Hint: they were his disciples. They were disciples because they were watching him and they were listening to him and they were mimicking him.

> *"You know, I saw Yeshua lay hands. Let me try that."*

Do you see?

> *"I saw Yeshua do that. Let me do that."*

A few years ago a popular fad was: "What would Yeshua or Jesus do?" Now you have people who are making wrist bands and T-shirts and all of that. Well, what would Yeshua do on the Sabbath? I know what he did!

As long as he was on the planet, it was his custom to enter, to go to worship on the Sabbath day. So if you don't want to do what Yeshua did, don't ask what Yeshua would do because he did not go to church on Sunday like a good little Christian boy!

He wasn't a Christian! Christianity hadn't even been invented yet!

> *The works that I do, you shall do also; and greater works than these shall he do; because I go unto my Father."*

You see, Yeshua kept the Sabbath! But it was not so that we don't have to! That's what folks are teaching.

> *"You know, well, he did that stuff so we don't have to do it."*

Well, he didn't eat pork, so you don't have to either!

That's just a little "chicken nugget" for you. [Laughter]

> **Luke 4:16** – *"And he came to Nazareth, where he had been brought up: and, as his custom was, he went into the synagogue on the sabbath day, and stood up for to read."*

He went into the synagogue as was his habit, his practice. Why would he do that? Because he believed that the commandments of YeHoVaH were for the people who called on the name of YeHoVaH. He believed that the people of the Kingdom did what the Kingdom required.

It's amazing how people of the world want to live in their neighborhood associations and want to hold everybody accountable to the neighborhood association rules and regulations. They want everybody to drive the speed limit. They want everybody to drive on "that" side of the road. They want everybody to let you in when you put that signal light on like their signal light means:

"Slow down and let me in."

And it is like:

"What planet are you from?"

Now, it's nice. We want to do the right thing. We do want to keep the law, but how can we advocate keeping man's law and reject keeping Father's law? I'll tell you exactly how you can do that. You live in one kingdom and that's the kingdom of this world. If you're advocating the laws of the kingdom of this world, then that's the only kingdom you're in. You had better get that.

If you're going to live in the Kingdom of YeHoVaH, you cannot live in the Kingdom of YeHoVaH and violate the law of the Kingdom. The only way you can reject the law of the Kingdom and advocate the laws of man is that you live in a manmade kingdom. And yeah, the man won't take you to jail because you're keeping the law, but wait until the Judgment.

It was his custom. It was expected that the new believers in Messiah would gather on the Sabbath and hear the scriptures read on the Sabbath day. Why? Because that was basically the only day they were pulled out and read. People were working all of the other six days. They didn't have their own little personal King James Bible.

There was probably one scroll in the whole city and guess where it was? It was in the place where they kept the scrolls. They didn't keep the scrolls in the Gentile temples. Oh, we're breaking it down today; like I said in the last section. It's going to be so simple that even a cave man will get it. They gathered on the Sabbath to read and to listen to the scriptures.

Those who refuse to keep the Law/Commandments are not of YeHoVaH.

It's that simple. No, you are NOT saved if you don't keep his commandments! Yeah, I said it! Now, do you have to keep his commandments to be saved? Absolutely not! Circumcision is not a requirement prior to salvation. Keeping the law is not a requirement. We don't keep the law so that we can be saved. We keep the law *because we are* [saved].

We are in the Kingdom of YeHoVaH. In his Kingdom he is King. In his Kingdom his law is the "Constitution" (for all you Constitution addicts).

You want to blame this President, you know? It's like:

> *"He just keeps violating the President and the Constitution of the United States — Ah!!!"*

Really? You have all of those so-called Constitutionalists allowing it. Do you hear what I'm saying? The Supreme Court is allowing it. The Judiciary branch and the Legislative branch of government are allowing the Executive branch to run roughshod over the nation. Really? So if you are going to blame one branch, you had better point the finger at the other two because they are all in it together. They are beating their war drums so you can send the some money.

> *"Oh, we don't care. Send us two dollars or three dollars or five dollars because we've got to get this person out."*

Yeah, so you can get somebody else in that is just like them! That's the law of the land. None of that matters in the Kingdom. It only matters here. The Kingdom of YeHoVaH is not a democracy. Don't think you are going to go up in there and vote. You might vote in your church. You might vote in your synagogue, but there will not be voting in the Kingdom. And I approve that message!

Many will say in that day:

> **Matthew 7:22** – *"Lord, Lord, have we not prophesied in thy name? and in thy name have cast out devils? and in thy name done many wonderful works?"*
>
> **Matthew 7:23** – *"And then will I profess unto them, 'I never knew you: depart from me, ye that work **<u>iniquity</u>**.'"*

The word there is *"anomia"* [*an-om-ee'-ah*] from illegality, i.e. violation of law or (genitive) wickedness: – iniquity, x transgress (-ion of) the law, unrighteousness.

"Get away from me, you law breakers!"

"Well, wait a minute. We don't have to keep the law!"

"Oh yeah? Says who?"

Your preacher. Your denomination. But you will not stand before your pastor, before your reverend, before your bishop, before your priest, before your father or before your apostle. **You will stand before Yeshua and he will say** (for those of you who feel like you don't have to keep the law):

"I don't know you!"

That's the word there. I didn't make this stuff up and I didn't put it there. Read it. It's in your Bible. Of course, your version might change the wording so that it doesn't have the impact, but he said:

"I will profess unto them."

Who?

"Those who are coming to me saying, 'Lord, Lord.'"

> *"Lord Jesus! Halleluyah! I finally made it."*

He says:

> *"Now, who are you?"*

[Arthur thumbs through the Bible to illustrate "Yeshua" searching for the person's name.]

> *"What's your name again? And you were born again on what date? Oh, you committed your life to the Lord early when you were of what age? You were a child?"*

[Arthur intently "searches" through the book and shakes the book. Then he looks in another book. Arthur Laughs.]

> *"I'm sorry but...but uh...Gabriel? Michael? We've got some trouble up in here. Clean up on aisle nine."*

They've "done" lost it.

> *"What do you mean I can't get in?! Out of all that I've done!"*

Oh yeah, you're going to have some folks "cutting up." You don't think you will? I can imagine!

> **1 John 3:4** – *"Whosoever committeth sin transgresseth also the law: for **sin** is the **transgression of the law**."*

Do you see this word here? Notice this word "anomia," which is the same word as "iniquity." When you go to *1 John 3:4*, the word "transgression of the law" is also "anomia" <458>.[4]

> *"Whosoever committeth sin transgresseth also the law: for sin is the transgression of the law."*

---

[4] This is reference number G458 (Greek) in the Strong's Concordance.

It's the same word. The 458 in the Strong's Concordance is the same word as "iniquity," or 458 in the Strong's Concordance. Transgression of the law is iniquity. Iniquity is the violation of the law. Of those who violate the law, Yeshua says:

> *"I don't know you."*
>
> *"What do you mean? We don't have to keep the law. You died so that we could be free from the law!"*
>
> *"Who told you that? Who told you that?"*
>
> *"Well, my preacher!"*
>
> *"Oh. You mean the one over there swimming? Splish-splash. He ain't taking no bath."*

Those who confess faith in Messiah but who refuse to keep the commandments are not of YeHoVaH.

> ***Revelation 12:17*** *– "And the dragon was wroth with the woman, and went to make war with the remnant of her seed, which keep the commandments of God, and have the testimony of Yeshua Messiah."*

You see, there are people out there who keep the commandments of God (as they know them); also known as the traditions of men, also known as the religion of the Jews. Let me tell you something, ladies and gentlemen. Every Sabbath there are synagogues around this city and cities around the United States and cities around the world where individuals are gathering and reading from the scrolls *and who reject Yeshua*.

> ***Revelation 14:12*** *– "Here is the patience of the saints:"*

Who are the saints?

> *"...here are they that keep the commandments of God, and the faith of Yeshua."*

DIETARY LAWS, CLEAN AND UNCLEAN

In *2 Corinthians chapter 6,* Paul writes:

> ***2 Corinthians 6:17*** *– "Wherefore come out from among them, and be ye separate, saith the Lord, and touch not the unclean thing; and I will receive you."*

Now, this seems very complex, but it's not complex. You see, the New Testament does not define what is clean. The New Testament does not define what is unclean. The New Testament does not define "food." There is no scripture in the New Testament that says what food is. As Americans, just as if you were Asian or if you were Hispanic or if you were of whatever culture, custom or nationality that you are; your diet, your eating will be based on the place where you grew up.

If you grew up eating monkey brains, if you grew up eating rats, if you grew up eating all kinds of – let me tell you something, ladies and gentlemen. There are people. I was talking to some people in a conference call just a few weeks ago and I wasn't thinking. I was thinking that I was talking to Americans.

You see, this is part of our problem sometimes because we are so accustomed to dealing with Americans. That's of course because as Americans who speak English, we are one of the only nations on the planet whose people [naturally] only speak one language. Many Americans have arrogance and feel that people should speak English.

> *"You should learn to speak English."*
>
> *"Oh yeah? And what gives you as an American the right to dictate the language of the world?"*

It is as if English is the language of the Kingdom. English is the "holy" language. Now there are people who are advocating that Hebrew is the language of the Kingdom, when the fact is that a very limited amount of people speak Hebrew. Those who say these things are teaching people the scriptures in English.

It just boggles my mind. I'm a simple person, but that boggles me. If that's the "holy" language, shouldn't you be teaching the Bible in that language? This is the holy book. There are people who believe that the language of the world should be English and guess what else? They believe that the currency of the world should be the U.S. dollar. Americans can be some very arrogant people.

I was talking to a Filipino, a pastor who was disputing the commands and I said:

> *"Do you know what? The Bible tells us what we are to believe, what we are to eat..."*

I said to him – and I was trying to be gross. I was trying to bring some shock value into the conversation. I said:

> *"Would you eat a rat?"*

Now, if I said that to one of you all, you would say:

> *"Eww!! No!!"*

This guy says:

> *"You know, some of my family members eat rats. There are people in our culture who eat rats."*

Do you know what I was thinking? I should have found something else to use as an example because this wasn't working. I had to regroup. Listen folks. There are people who eat things that we wouldn't even consider eating. **The culture that we live in determines the diet.**

I was talking to another couple. He's Caucasian and she's Filipino. I was talking about shellfish and she went off on me.

> *"In my culture, shellfish is a staple. We grew up on shellfish. What do you mean we can't eat shellfish?!"*

There are places where their culture and customs are opposite of the customs and culture of the Kingdom. Now what do you do? If you're only concerned about the kingdom of the world, you do nothing. But if you are concerned about the Kingdom of YeHoVaH, you are going to have to adapt. You're going to have to have a renewal of the mind. You are going to have to no longer be conformed to this world but be transformed.

You can come as you are, but you can't stay that way. He says:

> "Touch not the unclean thing and I will receive you."
>
> ***2 Corinthians 6:18*** – "'And [I] will be a Father unto you, and ye shall be my sons and daughters,' saith YeHoVaH."

Well, what if you touch the unclean thing? Will he be a Father to you? What if you eat the unclean thing? Will he be your Father? What are the unclean things? That's the first thing you need to think about.

> "What is he talking about with 'the unclean things?'"

I have asked many pastors and I'm telling you. People who are teaching this verse don't even know what they are saying. They don't even know what they are talking about.

> "What is the 'unclean thing' brother?"
>
> "I don't know. It's whatever Jesus called 'unclean.'"

Well, he called demons unclean and he cast demons out and they went into some unclean animals. What are those things called? What are they called? PIGS. You know, it's where you get the bacon from and the ham and the pork chops and the tenderloin.

I was thinking this morning. There are people who will eat rare steaks. I have yet to meet a person who will eat a rare pork chop or a rare pork roast.

> *"Aw, just let that blood ooze out onto the plate."*

It's amazing. They won't eat pork rare. Why? Because they know that there is something wrong with it! They know that if they eat it rare that they *will* get sick! It's not that they *might* get sick, they *will* get sick. But they don't think that way when they are eating that prime rib and that porterhouse and that T-bone and that filet mignon.

These are the sons and daughters who receive the promised Spirit of YeHoVaH.

> ***Acts 15:20*** *– "But that we write unto them, that they abstain from pollutions of idols, and from fornication, and from things strangled, and from blood."*

Let's break these down.

> ***Acts 15:21*** *– "For Moses of old time hath in every city them that preach him, being read in the synagogues every Sabbath day."*

It's unfortunate that in order for a person to hear the scriptures read, unless somehow they were able to get their own copy – let me tell you this. The Torah was a *very* protected book. It was a very, *very* protected book. It was protected because it contained the oracles of YeHoVaH and it was given to the Hebrew people. The Hebrew people didn't normally share it with non-Hebrew people.

So in order to hear the scrolls read; you had to be somewhere where they had scrolls being read. Unfortunately they were in the synagogues and in the temple. The beauty was when a Pharisee who may have had a copy or a Sadducee who may have had a copy was converted to Messiah. There are many in the Book of *Acts* that converted and that became believers.

We find them even here in *Acts 15* because these are Pharisees who are believers and who are still holding onto their Pharisee doctrine. You see, people walk in here [House Of Israel] from the Baptists, from the Methodists and from the Pentecostals. They bring their doctrines with them. It's the same with people joining us online. They are bringing their doctrines. Sometimes I say things that go against their doctrine and I get letters.

There are times when I say things here and I have conversations at the table. Even though people left the place that taught those doctrines, those doctrines are something they put their faith in. When you begin to address and attack or dismantle the doctrine, you dismantle the faith.

If you dismantle the faith, you have a person who doesn't know what to believe, what to think, what to stand on or what's right or what's wrong. They are confused now. So in some places they say:

> *"Oh yeah, you can come over here. Oh, you're a Gentile? Yeah, you can celebrate Christmas. Oh yeah, you can celebrate Easter. As a matter of fact, we have an Easter service. We have a Christmas service."*

Believe it or not, there are Messianic congregations that celebrate Christmas and Easter and Halloween! They celebrate all of that stuff and Rosh Hashanah in the seventh month and they keep a calendar that they know is incorrect.

This is what people do. **They hold onto their doctrines even when the facts have been presented.**

Abstain from pollutions of idols and **(567)** – the word there is "*ap-ekh-om-ahee*"; middle (reflexive) of **(568);** to hold oneself off, i.e. refrain: – abstain.

It really means "to abstain," "to hold oneself off," "to refrain." Basically, don't do it.

The word here "*i-do-loth'-oo-ton*" is a neuter of a compound of **(1497)** and a presumed derivative of **(2380)**; an *image-sacrifice,* i.e. part of an *idolatrous offering:* – (meat, thing that is) offered (in sacrifice, sacrificed) to (unto) idols.

Those of you who went with us through the teaching: *"Now Concerning Spiritual Gifts"* know that Paul was dealing with a lot of this idolatry. He was dealing with the different temples where they were bringing their sacrifices and offering certain parts of the animals. The remains of those animals that had parts that had been offered for sacrifice were sold in the meat markets; typically next to the temple.

People could go to the temple and get some cheap meat. It was like *Aldi's* or something, or *Save A Lot.* [5]

"Let's go and get some cloned meat."

I have to tell you something, ladies and gentlemen. As I was putting this together, it was like:

"Do you know what Arthur? You need to be a lot more specific and selective on where you get meat if you are going to eat it."

I can stand here and say:

"You know, if the church would just do this…"

And at the same time be convicted with:

"Well, why don't you do it?"

I mean, if these are the things that are commanded – meats that are sacrificed to idols. I don't go to a meat market that I know where there have been meats sacrificed to idols, but generally you don't know where the meat you get in the supermarkets came from.

---

[5] Aldi's and Save A Lot are American discount food stores.

"Oh brother, just eat what is put in front of you."

"Really? Really? Do you really want to take that?"

"As long as you don't tell me what it is."

"So you don't want to know? You don't want to know what you are putting in your temple?"

"Well, in some places, you're just violating their customs."

"Really? Do you think I'm more concerned about their customs than the Kingdom? Really?"

This is especially important if I'm sitting around in a restaurant and the food is being bought. Whatever they put in front of me? Just let your host order whatever they want you to eat? Really?

Abstain from fornication and **(4202)**. The word there is "*por-ni'-ah*"; from **(4203)** harlotry. This is including *adultery* and *incest*. Figuratively it is *idolatry:* – fornication, having sexual relationships without being married.

This is from where we get the words "pornography" and "pornographic." The word **(4203)** "*porn-yoo'-o*"; is from **(4204)** to *act* the *harlot,* i.e. (literal) *indulge* in unlawful *lust* (or either sex), or (figurative) *practice idolatry:* – commit (fornication).

What is "lawful" sex? Lawful sex doesn't mean that you have to use your credit card. There are some places where harlotry is legal. In Paul's day, they just went to the temples like Aphrodite's temple. They went to the temples and brought their sacrifices to Aphrodite and sacrificed and hung out with the priestesses. Then they went on about their way and that was their "spiritual act of worship."

Folks, you don't know. When you think about it, if your body is truly a temple and not just a temple but the temple of God; when you allow something unlawful to enter your temple, you have just defiled the temple. And guess what the Bible has to say about that?

Every sin that a man commits is outside of himself except fornication. **When a person commits fornication, they sin against their own temple.** They sin against themselves. That is the height of sin.

Abstain from things strangled or sexual sin. The word there is **(4155)**, "*pnee'-go*"; strengthened from **(4154)** to *wheeze,* i.e. (causative by implication) to *throttle* or *strangle* (*drown*): – choke, take by the throat.

It comes from **(4156)** – "*pnik-tos'*"; from **(4155)** *throttled,* i.e. (neuter concrete) an animal *choked* to death (*not bled*): – strangled. This word deals with not bleeding out. It is something that is killed and the blood is retained. If an animal is not bled out properly, then the blood remains in the animal. That is something that is strangled.

(WARNING: The next two paragraphs are fairly graphic.)

I remember. Man, I've got images. I remember when I was growing up and we had to slaughter a hog. As a child I remember this. My uncle had a farm and we had to get a sledge hammer. I am telling you. We tied that pig up and hit that pig in the head so many times. It refused to die. It was like you had to beat it to death with a sledge hammer. Then they would get a gun, a shot gun sometimes and shoot it. Now in some of these slaughter houses they have these slug guns or whatever and they just slug them.

But the proper way is to cut the throat. The animal bleeds out. It's humane, by the way. Now that I think about it, that pig squealed and if you didn't hit it in just the right place with the right amount of force; even a pig is YeHoVaH's creation.

Now look at some of the things they are shipping to us. Now they are cloning animals and they don't have to tell us! They are putting things in our supermarket aisles and we're going in there and paying top dollar for it. We have no idea how it's being slaughtered or whether it was properly slaughtered and we're buying it. I'm convicted.

Abstain from blood. The word is **(129)** – "*hah'ee-mah*"; of uncertain derivative; *blood,* literal (of men or animals), figurative (the *juice* of grapes) [of course we're not talking about the blood of grapes] or special (the atoning *blood* of Messiah); by implication *bloodshed,* also *kindred*: – blood.

It deals with two things: kindred and the blood of animals. This has led some to be split on this issue of whether or not this is dealing with murder or whether or not this is eating a rare steak (and it could be both). It's the shedding of blood. The life of course is definitely in the blood. There are people that feel that by eating the blood of their enemies, they gain their strength. There are some people who believe that by eating the blood of animals, there is something to it.

I remember sitting there with a friend of mine [having dinner] and that steak he was eating; man I'm telling you. That thing was swimming in blood. The meat was all red and bloody. I mean, it was like; I couldn't believe it. I'm watching him eat and I'm being grossed out. I'm trying not to puke while I eat. He was slurping it down. Blood was dripping down [points to his mouth] like a vampire. It was like:

"*Man, ugh."*

I had to turn my head. People eat like that and we're not supposed to. This gentleman was heavily into his church. He was a big supporter. He supported me. There are people who like their steaks rare "in the name of Jesus." This is New Testament. This is not Old Testament stuff, but it comes straight from the law. It's all law.

> *Acts 15:20* – *"But that we write unto them, that they abstain from pollutions of idols, and from fornication, and from things strangled, and from blood."*
>
> *Acts 15:21* – *"For Moses of old time hath in every city them that preach him, being read in the synagogues every Sabbath day."*

Again, **there are those who went versus those who were sent.** Let me show you.

> *Acts 15:24* – *"Forasmuch as **we have heard, that certain which <u>went</u> out from us have troubled you with words, subverting your souls,** saying, 'Ye must be circumcised, and keep the law: to **whom we gave no such commandment:**"*

Notice what they said: **certain which went out from us.** In *Acts 15:1,* this is important ladies and gentlemen. Believe me, this is important. It is certainly important for me. It says:

> *Acts 15:1* – *"And certain men which came down from Judaea taught the brethren, and said, 'Except ye be circumcised after the manner of Moses, ye cannot be saved.'"*

Where did they come from? They came down from Judaea. Who was in Judaea? The apostles. They came down from Judaea and possibly from Jerusalem. Imagine. Let me share something with you, okay? Listen to me. If someone came from Jerusalem today to speak to you in this place; if we invited somebody from Israel, from Jerusalem, people would be attending. This place would probably fill up.

> *"We've got a special speaker from Jerusalem."*

Oh, don't get quiet on me. I know. We just announce that thing and market that thing and you know.

> "We've got a Messianic Rabbi coming from the Holy Land."

People would be up in here:

> "I want to hear what he has to say!"

Yeah. Now, here it is and the Torah comes out from Jerusalem. In these lands, it's Syria. Antioch is in Syria. It's not in Israel. They came down from Jerusalem and they came to Antioch. This is where all of this takes place. Paul was a member of a congregation at Antioch and so was Barnabus and it was in Syria. They sent Paul and Barnabus up to Jerusalem to investigate what these individuals who came down were teaching. Here they came down and they are saying:

> "We are from Jerusalem. We had lunch with Peter and with James and we sat and fellowshipped. Let me tell you how wonderful and how beautiful it is to live in the land."

And it is like:

> "Wow! We get to meet some 'real' Jewish brothers! They're coming into our fellowship."

Do you see? But they had a couple of brothers in there who said:

> "Hold it! That's poppycock! That's nonsense! That's ridiculous! That's false!"

The Bible says that Paul and Barnabus had no small disputation. They stopped them. They said:

> "No!!"

Now, had Paul and Barnabus gone into their synagogue, they probably wouldn't have done that. But these came down to *their* place of worship. It's like somebody walking in *here*.

> "You're not coming up in here with that mess. No!"

So they've come down from Jerusalem and they're saying – look at verse 24.

> ***Acts 15:24** – "Forasmuch as **we have heard, that certain which <u>went</u> out from us…"***

They went out from *us*. They're claiming to be representatives from us! They're dropping *our* name! They're saying they are part of *our* ministry! *We* didn't send them!

I have had some people come here and I'm getting phone calls:

> *"Such and Such called me and they wanted me to help them promote their prophetic revelation and they told me that you had heard it and you loved the message."*

That's what I get (a phone call). I got two of those claiming to have come from me. People are dropping my name and I'm not that well known. I'm getting a call from a minister. If I'd mention his name, you'd know him. He called me, asking:

> *"Oh yeah, he was at your ministry…and he said…what can you tell me?"*

> *"I can tell you he's lying. I can tell you that I rejected the message and refused to listen to it because on the surface it was full of malarkey."*

But you see, these people bank on the fact that you're not going to make a connection. They are lying on me. So we have to be careful about who we endorse and who I put my name on. You are not going to go out of here saying that I sent you unless you have the right message. Notice what they said:

> ***Acts 15:24** – "Forasmuch as **we have heard, that certain which <u>went out from us</u> have troubled you with words, subverting your souls…"***

Words will subvert. Words will hurt. Words can cause confusion. Imagine somebody saying that according to biblical prophecy in Daniel's timeline, we've got a year and a half before a catastrophic event happens and we only have a short time to prepare ourselves. Then they put their countdown clock out there. They start sending out emails: "Day 1200...Day 1199...Day 200."

"Hooo-aaahhh!"

I really feel it impressed upon me and it has been for a couple of weeks that we have to deal with some false prophecy because it has started again. You would think that by Harold Camping leaving here that it would have stopped a lot of that mess. But it has just increased.

All you need is just one person to buy into it and then another person and another person and if you're hearing the same thing from five hundred people, it "must" be true. And if it's on the internet, it's "definitely" true. Right? Folks have their internet ministers. They are going from one internet broadcast to another internet broadcast.

> *"...saying, 'Ye must be circumcised, and keep the law:' to **whom we gave no such commandment:**"*

> *"We didn't tell them to teach that! We didn't give that commandment!"*

Now, were the apostles against the law? Because some would assume that by them saying:

> *"We gave no such commandment."*

Basically they are saying:

> *"We didn't send them."*

> ***Acts 15:25*** *– "It seemed good unto us, being assembled with one accord..."*

[They are saying]:

> *"Because of what they did, we all had to come together. These individuals go out and preach a message and now we all have to leave the business of advancing the Kingdom, and come down and have a meeting to decide how we're going to deal with those individuals who are going out teaching that message and causing problems among the Messianic community."*

There are people causing problems among the Messianic community right now. What are we supposed to do, just sit down and act like it's not happening?

> ***Acts 15:25*** *– "It seemed good unto us, being assembled with one accord, to send chosen men..."*

> *"Now we're going to send somebody. We didn't send them, but now we've got to send somebody."*

> *"...chosen men unto you with our beloved Barnabus and Paul,"*

> ***Acts 15:26*** *– "Men that have hazarded their lives for the name of our Lord Yeshua Messiah."*

> ***Acts 15:27*** *– "<u>We have sent</u> therefore..."*

> *"Here's who we're sending. We didn't send them, but we are sending these."*

> *"...Judas and Silas, who shall also tell you the same things by mouth."*

> *"We're going to send a letter. Our signatures are on it and they're going to tell you the same thing by mouth confirming it."*

> ***Acts 15:28*** *– "For it seemed good to the Holy Spirit..."*

"We didn't come up with this. This came from the Holy Spirit through the council of all of us coming together to deal with this issue that is causing problems and causing peoples' lives to be shipwrecked and whole families to be subverted by the words that they're speaking, claiming to have come from us."

Acts 15:28 *– "For it seemed good to the Holy Spirit, and to us, to lay upon you no greater burden than these necessary things;"*

Acts 15:29 *– "That ye abstain from meats offered to idols, and from blood, and from things strangled, and from fornication: from which if ye keep yourselves, ye shall do well. Fare ye well."*

KEEPING THE FEASTS

Paul kept the Feasts.

Acts 18:19 *– "And he came to Ephesus, and left them there: but he himself entered into the synagogue, and reasoned with the Jews."*

Acts 18:20 *– "When they desired him to tarry longer time with them, he consented not;"*

Acts 18:21 *– "But bade them farewell, saying, 'I must by all means keep this feast that cometh in Jerusalem: but I will return again unto you, if God will.' And he sailed from Ephesus."*

Now this word, this term is not in several versions of the Bible. It's not in the Amplified. It's not in the New International Version (NIV). There are a few versions that this phrase is not in and where it says:

"I must by all means keep this feast."

Paul is saying:

> *"I must by all means keep this feast that cometh in Jerusalem."*

He wasn't just keeping a feast. He was keeping a feast in Jerusalem. Why? It's because Jerusalem was the place where feasts were kept. Paul here in *Acts 18* is practicing keeping the feasts.

> *"Now, wait a minute. Why is Paul keeping the feasts? Didn't he teach that we shouldn't be... 'Let no man judge you concerning new moons and Sabbath days?' Didn't Paul say that?"*

What Paul was saying was that:

> *"Don't let anybody judge you because you keep the feasts. Don't let anybody judge you because you keep the Sabbaths, the high Sabbath days. Don't let any man judge you."*

But Christians have turned this thing around and said:

> *"Don't let anybody judge you because you don't keep the feasts."*

Paul wasn't writing to Christians! He was writing to individuals who did not have *Matthew, Mark, Luke, John* and *Acts*. They only had one set of scriptures (the Tanakh), and in the Tanakh, you kept the feasts! *Acts 20:16* shows us him:

> ***Acts 20:16*** – *"For Paul had determined to sail by Ephesus, because he would not spend the time in Asia: **for he hasted**, if it were possible for him, to be at Jerusalem the day of Pentecost."*

He was hastening.

> ***1 Corinthians 5:8*** – *"Therefore let us keep the feast,"*

He wrote in *1 Corinthians*. In *Acts* he is keeping them. In *1 Corinthians* he is writing to the Corinthians:

> ***1 Corinthians 5:8** – "Therefore let us keep the feast, not with old leaven, neither with the leaven of malice and wickedness; but with the unleavened bread of sincerity and truth."*

In other words, we don't keep the feasts like they of old kept the feasts. We're not dealing with all of that tradition. We're looking at it from a biblical perspective minus the traditions and with that which we can do.

The implication of Jude's letter is that they were keeping the feasts, but there were those who had the wrong spirit. There were false prophets and money-hungry ministers. There were talkers who knew not what they were talking about and this is what he wrote:

> ***Jude 1:12** – "These are spots in your **feasts** of charity, **when they feast with you**, feeding themselves without fear: clouds they are without water, carried about of winds; trees whose fruit withereth, without fruit, twice dead, plucked up by the roots;"*

Do you want to know who somebody is? Watch their fruit.

(See *"soon-yoo-o-kheh'-o"*; a derivative from **(4862)** meaning to *be in good condition*, i.e. [by implication] to *fare well*, or *feast*; to *entertain* sumptuously in company *with*, i.e. (middle or passive) to *revel together*: – feast with.)

This is the word here (from *Jude 1:12*) *"when they feast with you."* What kind of a feast are they feasting? They are feasting in the Feasts of YeHoVaH. What other feasts are there?

THE ESSENTIALS OF OUR FAITH IN CONCLUSION

The Essentials of Our Faith are:

*1. Faith in <u>**YeHoVaH**</u> and in the Messiah <u>**Yeshua/Yehoshua**</u> whom he sent*

2. Eating Biblically

3. Keeping the Sabbath

4. Keeping the Feasts

5. Baptism of the Holy Spirit

These are the essentials of our faith. Now, this is the end, "sort of, kind of." We're going to get into more of this in *Messianic 201*. We're going to be talking about adding to your faith; at least that is what I want to get into. But as I said, I have been compelled for the last several weeks to address some things that I'm hearing about among people that I know who are sincere and who desire to do what is right in the sight of YeHoVaH.

There are people who are out there; people who have developed a name. They have associated themselves with certain people and have used that name recognition to push an agenda that really is causing more fear. They use terms like:

"If you don't do this, there is no help for you."

"You will be judged."

"God is going to judge you."

"You will be doomed."

"You will not be prepared."

You see. These are things that are causing much fear and much angst among the brethren and there are a number of them. It goes from Jubilee to Daniel's timeline to "the end of the world is near." The whole [Doomsday] "prepper" movement has taken off. It's like wildfire spreading throughout the land. It's spreading throughout the nation. People don't know what to do; especially people who are living in apartment complexes or nursing homes. It's like they don't even realize the damage they are causing. You have people right now who are writing me.

> *"You know, I have to leave my state. I have to move because when that calamity hits, our state is targeted as one of the states that is going to be sunk."*

They are saying that certain parts of the United States are going to be submerged in water – whole states and cities wiped off the map. This stuff is moving around the internet and again, it is creating a lot of fear for a lot of people.

I have to tell you first and foremost that **if it's fear that it is creating, that is the first sign that it is not from YeHoVaH.** You see, YeHoVaH doesn't tell us stuff to cause us to be afraid or to fear. He tells us stuff to prepare us.

> *"Well, that's what we're doing. We're trying to warn you! Your blood is no longer on our hands!"*
>
> *"Good! You've said your piece; now go on about your business."*
>
> *"No! You have to preach this! You have to tell the people!!"*
>
> *"Oh, so now their blood is on my hands. Well, I'm going to do what I'm compelled to do and that is not to listen to you."*

Halleluyah somebody!

Enjoy These And Other Fine Teachings From Arthur Bailey Ministries

Check out our wide selection of important teachings that are also downloadable for FREE from our ministry website at www.ArthurBaileyMinistries.com. We have books, DVDs, videos, Discipleship and Leadership Training classes and more! Here is a sampling of our most popular teachings:

28 Blessings of Deuteronomy 28 — Summarizes the 28 blessings of *Deuteronomy 28* and what the blessings look like today. Learn how the blessings manifest and the importance of living a Torah-observant, Spirit-filled life. 4-DVDs. Approximately 5 hours.

Feast of Firstfruits — In this exciting teaching you will learn what are considered to be the Firstfruits offerings; when they are to be presented and why Firstfruits offerings are so important! You will also learn the prayer that is recited during this vital offering which assures the blessing of prosperity upon those who present these gifts unto YeHoVaH. Approximately 1.5 hours.

Hear, O Israel — "Hear, O Israel" is a call for ALL of the people of YeHoVaH to hear and to obey his commands. Oftentimes when people hear the word "Israel," they think "Jews." Israel consists of 12 tribes. The Jews are only one of those tribes. In this eye-opening, engaging and life-changing teaching, Arthur Bailey explains in-depth, Yeshua's response and the benefits of what it really means to hear and to obey! Approximately 2.5 hours in a 2-DVD set.

How To Hear God's Voice — Author and teacher Arthur Bailey shares important biblical truths to help you identify and distinguish the voice of the Almighty from every other voice. Learn why YeHoVaH communicates with his people, why he wants you to hear his voice, how to identify his voice from others, where he most likely speaks to you and so much more! 4-DVDs. Approximately 5.5 hours.

Relationships — Arthur Bailey presents from Scripture how the relationships in our lives must be categorized and prioritized according to their importance. You will learn the kind of relationship the Almighty wants with you, how to categorize and prioritize your relationships according to Scripture, how to identify and rectify wrong relationships and more. 2-DVDs. Approximately 2.5 hours.

Maximizing Your Talents — Understand the parable taught by Yeshua after sharing with his disciples about the Gospel of the Kingdom being preached to the whole world before the end comes. The parable is about three servants who were given specific talents. What distinguished the wise servant from the wicked servant in this parable was determined by what they did with the talents they had been given. Approximately 1.5 hours.

Merry Christmas? — Where did Christmas originate? What does the Bible have to say about Christmas and its relationship to the birth of Christ? Is Christmas even in the Bible? Should "Christ" be in Christmas? Is Jesus the reason for the season? How should true believers respond to Christmas? These questions and so many more will be answered in this timeless Christmas message. Approximately 1.5 hours.

The ReNEWed Covenant — In this teaching Arthur Bailey gives a clear, eye-opening, biblical explanation of what the New Covenant is and with whom it is made. He explains how Jews and Gentiles enter into this covenant and what it means for believers today. You will understand why it is called The ReNEWed Covenant and the significant power that is released within the lives of all who embrace the ReNEWed Covenant. This teaching will change your life forever! Approximately 1.5 hours.

The Power of the Holy Spirit — Author and teacher Arthur Bailey reveals the prerequisites all believers must meet to be filled with the Holy Spirit and power. What is this power that Yeshua spoke of? Is it still available for disciples of Yeshua today and how can they operate in it? These and many other questions will be answered in this fascinating, informative teaching series. 4-DVDs. Approximately 5.5 hours.

True Biblical Prosperity — What is prosperity? Is prosperity biblical? Is poverty a curse? Can believers be prosperous? What does the Bible teach about prosperity? What is true biblical prosperity? What you believe about prosperity will determine what you can and cannot receive from YeHoVaH. This teaching series will leave you with a wealth of information to help you understand why YeHoVaH wants his people to be *prosperous* and to know what *True Biblical Prosperity* looks like! 4-DVDs. Approximately 5.5 hours.

You Must Be Born Again — The church world took a conversation Yeshua had with a Pharisee at night, and built powerhouse ministries teaching a gospel message of "salvation" and altar calls. Many sermons have been taught about being "born again" and what it should mean to believers today. But what does *John 3:16* really teach within the context that it is written? Like many other biblical passages, this much-quoted verse is preached in a manner that has become isolated from the context in which it was originally written. Approximately 2.5 hours in a 2-DVD set.

The New Covenant — When did the New Covenant begin? Arthur Bailey journeys inside the first Jerusalem Council as the Apostles, Elders and Ruach Ha Kodesh (Holy Spirit) "discuss" how to deal with a false teaching circulating among believers. Arthur Bailey is a Spirit-filled, New Covenant minister who boldly teaches the Hebrew Roots of the Christian faith. He removes the confusion from covenants that are as important today as long ago. Two episodes.

The Baptism of the Holy Spirit — Yeshua said in *Acts* 1 verse 5: *"For John truly baptized with water; but ye shall be baptized with the Holy Ghost not many days hence."* In verse 8: *"But ye shall receive power, after that the Holy Ghost is come upon you: and ye shall be witnesses unto me both in Jerusalem, and in all Judea, and in Samaria, and unto the uttermost parts of the earth."* When we are baptized with the Holy Spirit, we receive power and authority to speak for YeHoVaH and to demonstrate his power! In this 4-DVD series learn the true evidence of the baptism of the Holy Spirit and more! A must-have for every true believer who wants to walk in their authority. Over 5 hours of teaching.

<u>The Fall Feasts Of YeHoVaH</u> — A 6-DVD set with over 6.5 hours of teaching. Includes teachings on the Feast of Trumpets/Yom Teruah, Day of Atonement/Yom Kippur, the Feast of Tabernacles/Sukkot and the Last Great Day/Shemini Atzeret. This introduction to the Fall Feasts provides insight and understanding of the prophetic shadow pictures of good things to come and helps us to understand how to celebrate these amazing days in a way that pleases Almighty YeHoVaH.

<u>Now Concerning Spiritual Gifts</u> — A 6-DVD set. Over 6.5 hours. Some suggest that the gifts of the Spirit have ceased operation and that the law is done away with. Among those who accept and teach that the spiritual gifts of the Bible are still operational today, many have abused and misused these gifts in their assembly; similar to the days of Corinth to whom Paul wrote to correct. This series removes the mystery over manifesting spiritual gifts and empowering believers.

<u>And The Heavens Were Opened</u> — An in-depth, inspiring journey through the feasts of Shavuot, Yom Teruah and Hanukkah. Reveals the importance of these biblical events for today's Spirit-filled believers in Yeshua. Learn about operating in the gifts of the Holy Spirit, the works of Messiah and the rededication of the 2nd temple at Hanukkah. 3-DVDs. About 4.5 hours.

<u>Keeping Torah Living Spirit Filled</u> — Journey inside the first Jerusalem Council. Explore how early leaders through the Ruach Ha Kodesh dealt with false teachings circulating among believers and how they incorporated Gentile converts into the newly formed Messianic community. Deepen your understanding. Strengthen your walk in Yeshua Messiah. 3 episodes in about 1.5 hous.

<u>The Love of God</u> — 4-DVDs. Paul wrote in the Book of Romans, *"But God commendeth his love toward us, in that, while we were yet sinners, Messiah died for us."* God demonstrated his love for us by giving his only begotten son to die for our sins. How can we show our love for God? Journey through the *greatest love story ever written.* Learn what our response to the love of God should be. A true story of love, of overcoming, of victory and of power. Approximately 5.5 hours.

Walking in the Power of the Holy Spirit; My Testimony — Join Arthur Bailey as he shares experiences and unique insights in this perceptive, sometimes hilarious and always instructive journey through his ministry spanning more than three decades. He generously shares his life-changing adventures of discovering and tapping back into the roots of the faith that he has long preached with boldness. As a former pastor and teacher in five different Christian denominations before coming to the true faith of the kingdom of YeHoVaH; his unique story is priceless and required listening for those who desire to enhance their own walk in Torah-obedience and in Yeshua Messiah. About 1.5 hours of teaching.

And You Shall Love The Lord — The creator of the universe demonstrated his love for us by sacrificing his only begotten son for the sins of man. The Love of God is a gift! You cannot earn it. You don't deserve it and you can't buy it. How do we demonstrate our love for God? Often when sharing the gospel of Yeshua (*the gospel Yeshua taught, not the gospel "about Jesus"*), the subject of the "law" comes up. Yeshua clearly stated that he did not come to do away with or to abolish the law (*Matthew 5:17*). Yet people still argue that we must only "love" YeHoVaH with all of our heart, mind, soul and strength. Are we doing that? What does this look like? The Bible tells us how YeHoVaH wants us to show our love for him. Find answers to questions that you won't find in religion. About 2.5 hours of teaching on 2-DVDs.

What Do We Do With Those Gentiles? — Discover how according to *Acts 15*, a major challenge existed which confronted the newly formed Messianic community. Arthur Bailey journeys inside the first Jerusalem Council where the Apostles, Elders and the Ruach Ha Kodesh "discussed" how to deal with false teachings and how to incorporate Gentile converts into the newly formed Messianic community. Jewish believers in Yeshua struggled with transitions from ethnic Jewish religious practices which included non-Hebrew people who were unfamiliar with the rich heritage and traditions formed by the Pharisees and handed down by the Elders. This teaching will deepen and strengthen your spiritual walk in Yeshua Messiah as you learn more about the history of the early called-out ones of faith. 2 episodes.

<u>**Messianic 201: "Adding to your Faith"**</u> — This is the second in a series of three introductory teachings. Messianic 201 picks up where Messianic 101 "The Essentials" leaves off. In this teaching you will learn the crucial elements that should be added to the believers' faith to keep from falling. This teaching is a must-have for anyone desiring to build their faith in Messiah Yeshua. About 2.5 hours of teaching in a 2-DVD set. Follow up with *Messianic 301 "Perfecting Your Faith."*

<u>**Messianic 301: "Perfecting Your Faith – Maturing in Messiah"**</u> — Today there is as much confusion about being "Messianic" as there is on certain issues across denominational Christianity. In "Messianic 301: Perfecting Your Faith –Maturing in Messiah,'" the teaching continues where Messianic 201: "Adding to your Faith" left off. This is the third installment of this phenomenal series which deals with perfecting the faith that we have been given. The series provides essential tools for maturing your faith in Messiah Yeshua. Over 5 hours of teaching on 4-DVDs.

Browse our Huge Selection of Teaching Resources

Check out our comprehensive collection of books, book/DVD combos, study tools, gifts and unpackaged teachings. There is something for everyone. Makes terrific gifts as well as study programs and witnessing tools for individuals or church ministries! Here is just a small sampling of our many books and educational materials:

Feast of Firstfruits	How To Hear God's Voice	It's Not Finished	Maximizing Your Talents
Sunday Is Not The Sabbath? (English)	Sunday Is Not The Sabbath? (Russian)	The Feast Of Pentecost	What About Grace?
Leadership Development	To Tithe or NOT To Tithe	The Book of Galatians A 4-Book set!	Discipleship Training

Discipleship Training & Leadership Development Programs

Enroll now in our FREE Discipleship Training and Leadership Development programs! These are the only Messianic Hebrew Roots of the faith programs like them on the planet! Learn more about the true history of the faith once delivered to the saints as you prepare for ministry and leadership services of any kind. The *Discipleship Training program* is our 105-class, 2-year accredited, Seminary-level program. Our 27-class *Leadership Development* course is for ministry and personal enrichment. For all believers regardless of your spiritual walk. All courses and materials are available online. Visit us at:

Discipleship101.tv   Leadership101.tv

Shalom!

You have just enjoyed one of the many fine teachings available through Arthur Bailey Ministries. Our full selection of materials are available at:

www.ArthurBaileyMinistries.com

Are you interested in learning more about the *True Gospel* and how to better communicate the word of YeHoVaH? Arthur Bailey Ministries now offers the world's first Messianic, Hebrew Roots of the Faith **Discipleship Training** and **Kingdom Leadership Development** programs. These exclusive learning opportunities are available in workbook and DVD formats and also online for individual or classroom study. Enroll for FREE today!

Discipleship101.tv   Leadership101.tv

Thank you for your interest in our products and ministry teachings! We invite you to participate in our fellowship services at House Of Israel in Charlotte; through one of our satellite locations, or via the Internet. Please see our web site for our weekly television broadcast schedule and live internet events. We are reaching, preaching, and teaching the *True Gospel of the Kingdom of YeHoVaH to the Whole World.* **We would be honored if you would join us!**

Fellowship Location
House Of Israel
1334 Hill Road
Charlotte, NC 28210

Mailing Address
Arthur Bailey Ministries
PO Box 49744
Charlotte, NC 28277

Office Phone
888-899-1479

Join us each week for our LIVE broadcasts
Thursdays @ 7pm ET • Saturdays @ 11am ET

Please stop in at our ministry web site to order any of the DVDs, books and other teaching materials and supplies available at our online store.

www.ArthurBaileyMinistries.com

In addition to placing your order online on our secure website, you may also call in your orders at 1-888-899-1479, or send your check or money order to:

Arthur Bailey Ministries
P.O. Box 49744
Charlotte, NC 28277

Your Support is Highly Appreciated!

Be Blessed in Yeshua Messiah! Shalom!

Taking the True Gospel of the Kingdom of YeHoVaH to the Whole World...

Made in the USA
Columbia, SC
23 August 2023